THE PELICAN SHAKESPEARE
GENERAL EDITORS

STEPHEN ORGEL
A. R. BRAUNMULLER

Twelfth Night

Ellen Terry as Viola, 1884

William Shakespeare

———

Twelfth Night
or
What You Will

EDITED BY JONATHAN CREWE

PENGUIN BOOKS

PENGUIN BOOKS

Published by the Penguin Group

Penguin Group (USA) Inc., 375 Hudson Street, New York, New York 10014, U.S.A.

Penguin Group (Canada), 90 Eglinton Avenue East, Suite 700, Toronto, Ontario,
Canada M4P 2Y3 (a division of Pearson Penguin Canada Inc.)

Penguin Books Ltd, 80 Strand, London WC2R 0RL, England

Penguin Ireland, 25 St Stephen's Green, Dublin 2, Ireland (a division of Penguin Books Ltd)

Penguin Group (Australia), 250 Camberwell Road, Camberwell, Victoria 3124,
Australia (a division of Pearson Australia Group Pty Ltd)

Penguin Books India Pvt Ltd., 11 Community Centre,
Panchsheel Park, New Delhi – 110 017, India

Penguin Group (NZ), 67 Apollo Drive, Mairangi Bay,
Auckland 1311, New Zealand (a division of Pearson New Zealand Ltd.)

Penguin Books (South Africa) (Pty) Ltd, 24 Sturdee Avenue,
Rosebank, Johannesburg 2196, South Africa

Penguin Books Ltd, Registered Offices: 80 Strand, London WC2R 0RL, England

Twelfth Night, or, What You Will edited by Charles T. Prouty
published in the United States of America in Penguin Books
1958
Revised edition published 1972
This new edition edited by Jonathan Crewe published 2000

20 19 18 17 16

ISBN 978-0-14-071489-0

Printed in the United States of America
Set in Garamond
Designed by Virginia Norey

Contents

Publisher's Note

IT IS ALMOST half a century since the first volumes of the
Pelican Shakespeare appeared under the general editorship
of Alfred Harbage. The fact that a new edition, rather
than simply a revision, has been undertaken reflects the
profound changes textual and critical studies of Shakespeare have undergone in the past twenty years. For the
new Pelican series, the texts of the plays and poems have
been thoroughly revised in accordance with recent schol-
arship, and in some cases have been entirely reedited. New
introductions and notes have been provided in all the volumes. But the new Shakespeare is also designed as a successor to the original series; the previous editions have
been taken into account, and the advice of the previous
editors has been solicited where it was feasible to do so.

Certain textual features of the new Pelican Shakespeare
should be particularly noted. All lines are numbered that
contain a word, phrase, or allusion explained in the
glossarial notes. In addition, for convenience, every tenth
line is also numbered, in italics when no annotation is indicated. The intrusive and often inaccurate place headings
inserted by early editors are omitted (as is becoming standard practice), but for the convenience of those who miss
them, an indication of locale now appears as the first item
in the annotation of each scene.

In the interest of both elegance and utility, each speech
prefix is set in a separate line when the speaker's lines are
in verse, except when those words form the second half of
a verse line. Thus the verse form of the speech is kept vi-
sually intact. What is printed as verse and what is printed
as prose has, in general, the authority of the original texts.
Departures from the original texts in this regard have only
the authority of editorial tradition and the judgment of
the Pelican editors; and, in a few instances, are admittedly
arbitrary.

The Theatrical World

Economic realities determined the theatrical world in which Shakespeare's plays were written, performed, and received. For centuries in England, the primary theatrical tradition was nonprofessional. Craft guilds (or "mysteries") provided religious drama – mystery plays – as part of the celebration of religious and civic festivals, and schools and universities staged classical and neoclassical drama in both Latin and English as part of their curricula. In these forms, drama was established and socially acceptable. Professional theater, in contrast, existed on the margins of society. The acting companies were itinerant; playhouses could be any available space – the great halls of the aristocracy, town squares, civic halls, inn yards, fair booths, or open fields – and income was sporadic, dependent on the passing of the hat or on the bounty of local patrons. The actors, moreover, were considered little better than vagabonds, constantly in danger of arrest or expulsion.

In the late 1560s and 1570s, however, English professional theater began to gain respectability. Wealthy aristocrats fond of drama – the Lord Admiral, for example, or the Lord Chamberlain – took acting companies under their protection so that the players technically became members of their households and were no longer subject to arrest as homeless or masterless men. Permanent theaters were first built at this time as well, allowing the companies to control and charge for entry to their performances.

Shakespeare's livelihood, and the stunning artistic explosion in which he participated, depended on pragmatic and architectural effort. Professional theater requires ways to restrict access to its offerings; if it does not, and admission fees cannot be charged, the actors do not get paid, the costumes go to a pawnbroker, and there is no such thing as a professional, ongoing theatrical tradition. The answer to that economic need arrived in the late 1560s and 1570s with the creation of the so-called public or amphitheater playhouse. Recent discoveries indicate that the precursor of the Globe playhouse in London (where Shakespeare's mature plays were presented) and the Rose theater (which presented Christopher Marlowe's plays and some of Shakespeare's earliest ones) was the Red Lion theater of 1567. Archaeological studies of the foundations of the Rose and Globe theaters have revealed that the open-air theater of the 1590s and later was probably a polygonal building with fourteen to twenty or twenty-four sides, multistoried, from 75 to 100 feet in diameter, with a raised, partly covered "thrust" stage that projected into a group of standing patrons, or "groundlings," and a covered gallery, seating up to 2,500 or more (very crowded) spectators.

These theaters might have been about half full on any given day, though the audiences were larger on holidays or when a play was advertised, as old and new were, through printed playbills posted around London. The metropolitan area's late-Tudor, early-Stuart population (circa 1590-1620) has been estimated at about 150,000 to 250,000. It has been supposed that in the mid-1590s there were about 15,000 spectators per week at the public theaters; thus, as many as 10 percent of the local population went to the theater regularly. Consequently, the theaters' repertories – the plays available for this experienced and frequent audience – had to change often: in the month between September 15 and October 15, 1595, for instance, the Lord Admiral's Men performed twenty-eight times in eighteen different plays.

Since natural light illuminated the amphitheaters' stages, performances began between noon and two o'clock and ran without a break for two or three hours. They often concluded with a jig, a fencing display, or some other nondramatic exhibition. Weather conditions determined the season for the amphitheaters: plays were performed every day (including Sundays, sometimes, to clerical dismay) except during Lent – the forty days before Easter – or periods of plague, or sometimes during the summer months when law courts were not in session and the most affluent members of the audience were not in London.

To a modern theatergoer, an amphitheater stage like that of the Rose or Globe would appear an unfamiliar mixture of plainness and elaborate decoration. Much of the structure was carved or painted, sometimes to imitate marble; elsewhere, as under the canopy projecting over the stage, to represent the stars and the zodiac. Appropriate painted canvas pictures (of Jerusalem, for example, if the play was set in that city) were apparently hung on the wall behind the acting area, and tragedies were accompanied by black hangings, presumably something like crepe festoons or bunting. Although these theaters did not employ what we would call scenery, early modern spectators saw numerous large props, such as the "bar" at which a prisoner stood during a trial, the "mossy bank" where lovers reclined, an arbor for amorous conversation, a chariot, gallows, tables, trees, beds, thrones, writing desks, and so forth. Audiences might learn a scene's location from a sign (reading "Athens," for example) carried across the stage (as in Bertolt Brecht's twentieth-century productions). Equally captivating (and equally irritating to the theater's enemies) were the rich costumes and personal props the actors used: the most valuable items in the surviving theatrical inventories are the swords, gowns, robes, crowns, and other items worn or carried by the performers.

Magic appealed to Shakespeare's audiences as much as it does to us today, and the theater exploited many deceptive and spectacular devices. A winch in the loft above the stage, called "the heavens," could lower and raise actors playing gods, goddesses, and other supernatural figures to and from the main acting area, just as one or more trapdoors permitted entrances and exits to and from the area, called "hell," beneath the stage. Actors wore elementary makeup such as wigs, false beards, and face paint, and they employed pig's bladders filled with animal blood to make wounds seem more real. They had rudimentary but effective ways of pretending to behead or hang a person. Supernumeraries (stagehands or actors not needed in a particular scene) could make thunder sounds (by shaking a metal sheet or rolling an iron ball down a chute) and show lightning (by blowing inflammable resin through tubes into a flame). Elaborate fireworks enhanced the effects of dragons flying through the air or imitated such celestial phenomena as comets, shooting stars, and multiple suns. Horses' hoofbeats, bells (located perhaps in the tower above the stage), trumpets and drums, clocks, cannon shots and gunshots, and the like were common sound effects. And the music of viols, cornets, oboes, and recorders was a regular feature of theatrical performances.

For two relatively brief spans, from the late 1570s to 1590 and from 1599 to 1614, the amphitheaters competed with the so-called private, or indoor, theaters, which originated as, or later represented themselves as, educational institutions training boys as singers for church services and court performances. These indoor theaters had two features that were distinct from the amphitheaters': their personnel and their playing spaces. The amphitheaters' adult companies included both adult men, who played the male roles, and boys, who played the female roles; the private, or indoor, theater companies, on the other hand, were entirely composed of boys aged about 8 to 16, who were, or could pretend to be, candidates for singers in a church or a royal boys' choir. (Until 1660, professional theatrical companies included no women.) The playing space would appear much more familiar to modern audiences than the long-vanished amphitheaters; the later indoor theaters were, in fact, the ancestors of the typical modern theater. They were enclosed spaces, usually rectangular, with the stage filling one end of the rectangle and the audience arrayed in seats or benches across (and sometimes lining) the building's longer axis. These spaces staged plays less frequently than the public theaters (perhaps only once a week) and held far fewer spectators than the amphitheaters: about 200 to 600, as opposed to 2,500 or more. Fewer patrons mean a smaller gross income, unless each pays more. Not surprisingly, then, private theaters charged higher prices than the amphitheaters, probably sixpence, as opposed to a penny for the cheapest entry.

Protected from the weather, the indoor theaters presented plays later in the day than the amphitheaters, and used artificial illumination – candles in sconces or candelabra. But candles melt, and need replacing, snuffing, and trimming, and these practical requirements may have been part of the reason the indoor theaters introduced breaks in the performance, the intermission so dear to the heart of theatergoers and to the pocketbooks of theater concessionaires ever since. Whether motivated by the need to tend to the candles or by the entrepreneurs' wishing to sell oranges and liquor, or both, the indoor theaters eventually established the modern convention of the non-continuous performance. In the early modern "private" theater, musical performances apparently filled the intermissions, which in Stuart theater jargon seem to have been called "acts."

At the end of the first decade of the seventeenth century, the distinction between public amphitheaters and private indoor companies ceased. For various cultural, political, and economic reasons, individual companies gained control of both the public, open-air theaters and the indoor ones, and companies mixing adult men and boys took over the formerly "private" theaters. Despite the death of the boys' companies and of their highly innovative theaters (for which such luminous playwrights as Ben Jonson, George Chapman, and John Marston wrote), their playing spaces and conventions had an immense impact on subsequent plays: not merely for the intervals (which stressed the artistic and architectonic importance

of "acts"), but also because they introduced political and
social satire as a popular dramatic ingredient, even in
tragedy, and a wider range of actorly effects, encouraged
by their more intimate playing spaces.

Even the briefest sketch of the Shakespearean theatrical
world would be incomplete without some comment on the
social and cultural dimensions of theaters and playing in
the period. In an intensely hierarchical and status-
conscious society, professional actors and their ventures had
hardly any respectability; as we have indicated, to protect
themselves against laws designed to curb vagabondage and
the increase of masterless men, actors resorted to the near-
fiction that they were the servants of noble masters, and
wore their distinctive livery. Hence the company for which
Shakespeare wrote in the 1590s called itself the Lord
Chamberlain's Men and pretended that the public, money-
getting performances were in fact rehearsals for private performances before that high court official. From 1598, the
Privy Council had licensed theatrical companies, and after
1603, with the accession of King James I, the companies
gained explicit royal protection, just as the Queen's Men
had for a time under Queen Elizabeth. The Chamberlain's
Men became the King's Men, and the other companies
were patronized by the other members of the royal family.

These designations were legal fictions that half-
concealed an important economic and social development, the evolution away from the theater's organization
on the model of the guild, a self-regulating confraternity
of individual artisans, into a proto-capitalist organization.
Shakespeare's company became a joint-stock company,
where persons who supplied capital and, in some cases,
such as Shakespeare's, capital and talent, employed themselves and others in earning a return on that capital. This
development meant that actors and theater companies
were outside both the traditional guild structures, which
required some form of civic or royal charter, and the feu-
dal household organization of master-and-servant. This
anomalous, maverick social and economic condition

made theater companies practically unruly and potentially even dangerous; consequently, numerous official
bodies – including the London metropolitan and ecclesi-
astical authorities as well as, occasionally, the royal court
itself – tried, without much success, to control and even
to disband them.

Public officials had good reason to want to close the
theaters: they were attractive nuisances – they drew often
riotous crowds, they were always noisy, and they could be
politically offensive and socially insubordinate. Until the
Civil War, however, anti-theatrical forces failed to shut
down professional theater, for many reasons – limited
surveillance and few police powers, tensions or outright
hostilities among the agencies that sought to check or
channel theatrical activity, and lack of clear policies for
control. Another reason must have been the theaters' un-
deniable popularity. Curtailing any activity enjoyed by
such a substantial percentage of the population was difficult, as various Roman emperors attempting to limit cir-
cuses had learned, and the Tudor-Stuart audience was not
merely large, it was socially diverse and included women.
The prevalence of public entertainment in this period
has been underestimated. In fact, fairs, holidays, games,
sporting events, the equivalent of modern parades, freak
shows, and street exhibitions all abounded, but the theater was the most widely and frequently available entertainment to which people of every class had access. That
fact helps account both for its quantity and for the fear
and anger it aroused.

WILLIAM SHAKESPEARE OF
STRATFORD-UPON-AVON, GENTLEMAN

Many people have said that we know very little about
William Shakespeare's life – pinheads and postcards are
often mentioned as appropriately tiny surfaces on which
to record the available information. More imaginatively

and perhaps more correctly, Ralph Waldo Emerson wrote, "Shakespeare is the only biographer of Shakespeare. . . . So far from Shakespeare's being the least known, he is the one person in all modern history fully known to us."

In fact, we know more about Shakespeare's life than we do about almost any other English writer's of his era. His last will and testament (dated March 25, 1616) survives, as do numerous legal contracts and court documents involving Shakespeare as principal or witness, and parish records in Stratford and London. Shakespeare appears quite often in official records of King James's royal court, and of course Shakespeare's name appears on numerous title pages and in the written and recorded words of his literary contemporaries Robert Greene, Henry Chettle, Francis Meres, John Davies of Hereford, Ben Jonson, and many others. Indeed, if we make due allowance for the bloating of modern, run-of-the-mill bureaucratic records, more information has survived over the past four hundred years about William Shakespeare of Stratford-upon-Avon, Warwickshire, than is likely to survive in the next four hundred years about any reader of these words.

What we do not have are entire categories of information – Shakespeare's private letters or diaries, drafts and revisions of poems and plays, critical prefaces or essays, commendatory verse for other writers' works, or instructions guiding his fellow actors in their performances, for instance – that we imagine would help us understand and appreciate his surviving writings. For all we know, many such data never existed as written records. Many literary and theatrical critics, not knowing what might once have existed, more or less cheerfully accept the situation; some even make a theoretical virtue of it by claiming that such data are irrelevant to understanding and interpreting the plays and poems.

So, what do we know about William Shakespeare, the man responsible for thirty-seven or perhaps more plays, more than 150 sonnets, two lengthy narrative poems, and some shorter poems?

While many families by the name of Shakespeare (or some variant spelling) can be identified in the English Midlands as far back as the twelfth century, it seems likely that the dramatist's grandfather, Richard, moved to Snitterfield, a town not far from Stratford-upon-Avon, sometime before 1529. In Snitterfield, Richard Shakespeare leased farmland from the very wealthy Robert Arden. By 1552, Richard's son John had moved to a large house on Henley Street in Stratford-upon-Avon, the house that stands today as "The Birthplace." In Stratford, John Shakespeare traded as a glover, dealt in wool, and lent money at interest; he also served in a variety of civic posts, including "High Bailiff," the municipality's equivalent of mayor. In 1557, he married Robert Arden's youngest daughter, Mary. Mary and John had four sons – William was the oldest – and four daughters, of whom only Joan outlived her most celebrated sibling. William was baptized (an event entered in the Stratford parish church records) on April 26, 1564, and it has become customary, without any good factual support, to suppose he was born on April 23, which happens to be the feast day of Saint George, patron saint of England, and is also the date on which he died, in 1616. Shakespeare married Anne Hathaway in 1582, when he was eighteen and she was twenty-six; their first child was born five months later. It has been generally assumed that the marriage was enforced and subsequently unhappy, but these are only assumptions; it has been estimated, for instance, that up to one third of Elizabethan brides were pregnant when they married. Anne and William Shakespeare had three children: Susanna, who married a prominent local physician, John Hall; and the twins Hamnet, who died young in 1596, and Judith, who married Thomas Quiney – apparently a rather shady individual. The name Hamnet was unusual but not unique: he and his twin sister were named for their godparents, Shakespeare's neighbors Hamnet and Judith Sadler. Shakespeare's father died in 1601 (the year of *Hamlet*), and Mary Arden Shakespeare died in 1608 (the year of *Coriolanus*). William Shakespeare's last surviving direct descendant was his granddaughter Elizabeth Hall, who died in 1670.

Between the birth of the twins in 1585 and a clear reference to Shakespeare as a practicing London dramatist in Robert Greene's sensationalizing, satiric pamphlet, *Greene's Groatsworth of Wit* (1592), there is no record of where William Shakespeare was or what he was doing. These seven so-called lost years have been imaginatively filled by scholars and other students of Shakespeare: some think he traveled to Italy, or fought in the Low Countries, or studied law or medicine, or worked as an apprentice actor/writer, and so on to even more fanciful possibilities. Whatever the biographical facts for those "lost" years, Greene's nasty remarks in 1592 testify to professional envy and to the fact that Shakespeare already had a successful career in London. Speaking to his fellow playwrights, Greene warns both generally and specifically:

> . . . trust them [actors] not: for there is an upstart crow, beautified with our feathers, that with his tiger's heart wrapped in a player's hide supposes he is as well able to bombast out a blank verse as the best of you; and being an absolute Johannes Factotum, is in his own conceit the only Shake-scene in a country.

The passage mimics a line from *3 Henry VI* (hence the play must have been performed before Greene wrote) and seems to say that "Shake-scene" is both actor and playwright, a jack-of-all-trades. That same year, Henry Chettle protested Greene's remarks in *Kind-Heart's Dream,* and each of the next two years saw the publication of poems – *Venus and Adonis* and *The Rape of Lucrece,* respectively – publicly ascribed to (and dedicated by) Shakespeare. Early in 1595 he was named one of the senior members of a prominent acting company, the Lord Chamberlain's Men, when they received payment for court performances during the 1594 Christmas season.

Clearly, Shakespeare had achieved both success and reputation in London. In 1596, upon Shakespeare's application, the College of Arms granted his father the now-familiar coat of arms he had taken the first steps to obtain almost twenty years before, and in 1598, John's son – now permitted to call himself "gentleman" – took a 10 percent share in the new Globe playhouse. In 1597, he bought a substantial bourgeois house, called New Place, in Stratford – the garden remains, but Shakespeare's house, several times rebuilt, was torn down in 1759 – and over the next few years Shakespeare spent large sums buying land and making other investments in the town and its environs. Though he worked in London, his family remained in Stratford, and he seems always to have considered Stratford the home he would eventually return to. Something approaching a disinterested appreciation of Shakespeare's popular and professional status appears in Francis Meres's *Palladis Tamia* (1598), a not especially imaginative and perhaps therefore persuasive record of literary reputations. Reviewing contemporary English writers, Meres lists the titles of many of Shakespeare's plays, including one not now known, *Love's Labor's Won,* and praises his "mellifluous & hony-tongued" "sugred Sonnets," which were then circulating in manuscript (they were first collected in 1609). Meres describes Shakespeare as "one of the best" English playwrights of both comedy and tragedy. In *Remains . . . Concerning Britain* (1605), William Camden – a more authoritative source than the imitative Meres – calls Shakespeare one of the "most pregnant witts of these our times" and joins him with such writers as Chapman, Daniel, Jonson, Marston, and Spenser. During the first decades of the seventeenth century, publishers began to attribute numerous play quartos, including some non-Shakespearean ones, to Shakespeare, either by name or initials, and we may assume that they deemed Shakespeare's name and supposed authorship, true or false, commercially attractive.

For the next ten years or so, various records show

Shakespeare's dual career as playwright and man of the theater in London, and as an important local figure in Stratford. In 1608-9 his acting company – designated the "King's Men" soon after King James had succeeded Queen Elizabeth in 1603 – rented, refurbished, and opened a small interior playing space, the Blackfriars theater, in London, and Shakespeare was once again listed as a substantial sharer in the group of proprietors of the playhouse. By May 11, 1612, however, he describes himself as a Stratford resident in a London lawsuit – an indication that he had withdrawn from day-to-day professional activity and returned to the town where he had always had his main financial interests. When Shakespeare bought a substantial residential building in London, the Blackfriars Gatehouse, close to the theater of the same name, on March 10, 1613, he is recorded as William Shakespeare "of Stratford upon Avon in the county of Warwick, gentleman," and he named several London residents as the building's trustees. Still, he continued to participate in theatrical activity: when the new Earl of Rutland needed an allegorical design to bear as a shield, or *impresa,* at the celebration of King James's Accession Day, March 24, 1613, the earl's accountant recorded a payment of 44 shillings to Shakespeare for the device with its motto.

For the last few years of his life, Shakespeare evidently concentrated his activities in the town of his birth. Most of the final records concern business transactions in Stratford, ending with the notation of his death on April 23, 1616, and burial in Holy Trinity Church, Stratford-upon-Avon.

THE QUESTION OF AUTHORSHIP

The history of ascribing Shakespeare's plays (the poems do not come up so often) to someone else began, as it continues, peculiarly. The earliest published claim that someone else wrote Shakespeare's plays appeared in an 1856 article by Delia Bacon in the American journal *Putnam's Monthly* – although an Englishman, Thomas Wilmot, had shared his doubts in private (even secretive) conversations with friends near the end of the eighteenth century. Bacon's was a sad personal history that ended in madness and poverty, but the year after her article, she published, with great difficulty and the bemused assistance of Nathaniel Hawthorne (then United States Consul in Liverpool, England), her *Philosophy of the Plays of Shakspere Unfolded.* This huge, ornately written, confusing farrago is almost unreadable; sometimes its intents, to say nothing of its arguments, disappear entirely beneath near-raving, ecstatic writing. Tumbled in with much supposed "philosophy" appear the claims that Francis Bacon (from whom Delia Bacon eventually claimed descent), Walter Ralegh, and several other contemporaries of Shakespeare's had written the plays. The book had little impact except as a ridiculed curiosity.

Once proposed, however, the issue gained momentum among people whose conviction was the greater in proportion to their ignorance of sixteenth- and seventeenth-century English literature, history, and society. Another American amateur, Catherine P. Ashmead Windle, made the next influential contribution to the cause when she published *Report to the British Museum* (1882), wherein she promised to open "the Cipher of Francis Bacon," though what she mostly offers, in the words of S. Schoenbaum, is "demented allegorizing." An entire new cottage industry grew from Windle's suggestion that the texts contain hidden, cryptographically discoverable ciphers – "clues" – to their authorship; and today there are not only books devoted to the putative ciphers, but also pamphlets, journals, and newsletters.

Although Baconians have led the pack of those seeking a substitute Shakespeare, in *"Shakespeare" Identified* (1920), J. Thomas Looney became the first published

"Oxfordian" when he proposed Edward de Vere, seventeenth earl of Oxford, as the secret author of Shakespeare's plays. Also for Oxford and his "authorship" there are today dedicated societies, articles, journals, and books. Less popular candidates – Queen Elizabeth and Christopher Marlowe among them – have had adherents, but the movement seems to have divided into two main contending factions, Baconian and Oxfordian. (For further details on all the candidates for "Shakespeare," see S. Schoenbaum, *Shakespeare's Lives,* 2nd ed., 1991.)

The Baconians, the Oxfordians, and supporters of other candidates have one trait in common – they are snobs. Every pro-Bacon or pro-Oxford tract sooner or later claims that the historical William Shakespeare of Stratford-upon-Avon could not have written the plays because he could not have had the training, the university education, the experience, and indeed the imagination or background their author supposedly possessed. Only a learned genius like Bacon or an aristocrat like Oxford could have written such fine plays. (As it happens, lucky male children of the middle class had access to better education than most aristocrats in Elizabethan England – and Oxford was not particularly well educated.) Shakespeare received in the Stratford grammar school a formal education that would daunt many college graduates today; and popular rival playwrights such as the very learned Ben Jonson and George Chapman, both of whom also lacked university training, achieved great artistic success, without being taken as Bacon or Oxford.

Besides snobbery, one other quality characterizes the authorship controversy: lack of evidence. A great deal of testimony from Shakespeare's time shows that Shakespeare wrote Shakespeare's plays and that his contemporaries recognized them as distinctive and distinctly superior. (Some of that contemporary evidence is collected in E. K. Chambers, *William Shakespeare: A Study of Facts and Problems,* 2 vols., 1930.) Since that testimony comes from Shakespeare's enemies and theatrical competitors as well as from his co-workers and from the Elizabethan equivalent of literary journalists, it seems unlikely that, if any one of these sources had known he was a fraud, they would have failed to record that fact.

Books About Shakespeare's Theater

Useful scholarly studies of theatrical life in Shakespeare's day include: G. E. Bentley, *The Jacobean and Caroline Stage,* 7 vols. (1941-68), and the same author's *The Professions of Dramatist and Player in Shakespeare's Time, 1590-1642* (1986); E. K. Chambers, *The Elizabethan Stage,* 4 vols. (1923); R. A. Foakes, *Illustrations of the English Stage, 1580-1642* (1985); Andrew Gurr, *The Shakespearean Stage,* 3rd ed. (1992), and the same author's *Play-going in Shakespeare's London,* 2nd ed. (1996); Edwin Nungezer, *A Dictionary of Actors* (1929); Carol Chillington Rutter, ed., *Documents of the Rose Playhouse* (1984).

Books About Shakespeare's Life

The following books provide scholarly, documented accounts of Shakespeare's life: G. E. Bentley, *Shakespeare: A Biographical Handbook* (1961); E. K. Chambers, *William Shakespeare: A Study of Facts and Problems,* 2 vols. (1930); S. Schoenbaum, *William Shakespeare: A Compact Documentary Life* (1977); and *Shakespeare's Lives,* 2nd ed. (1991), by the same author. Many scholarly editions of Shakespeare's complete works print brief compilations of essential dates and events. References to Shakespeare's works up to 1700 are collected in C. M. Ingleby et al., *The Shakespeare Allusion-Book,* rev. ed., 2 vols. (1932).

The Texts of Shakespeare

As FAR AS WE KNOW, only one manuscript conceivably in Shakespeare's own hand may (and even this is much disputed) exist: a few pages of a play called *Sir Thomas More*, which apparently was never performed. What we do have, as later readers, performers, scholars, students, are printed texts. The earliest of these survive in two forms: quartos and folios. Quartos (from the Latin for "four") are small books, printed on sheets of paper that were then folded in fours, to make eight double-sided pages. When these were bound together, the result was a squarish, eminently portable volume that sold for the relatively small sum of sixpence (translating in modern terms to about $5.00). In folios, on the other hand, the sheets are folded only once, in half, producing large, impressive volumes taller than they are wide. This was the format for important works of philosophy, science, theology, and literature (the major precedent for a folio Shakespeare was Ben Jonson's *Works,* 1616). The decision to print the works of a popular playwright in folio is an indication of how far up on the social scale the theatrical profession had come during Shakespeare's lifetime. The Shakespeare folio was an expensive book, selling for between fifteen and eighteen shillings, depending on the binding (in modern terms, from about $150 to $180). Twenty Shakespeare plays of the thirty-seven that survive first appeared in quarto, seventeen of which appeared during Shakespeare's lifetime; the rest of the plays are found only in folio.

The First Folio was published in 1623, seven years after Shakespeare's death, and was authorized by his fellow actors, the co-owners of the King's Men. This publication was certainly a mark of the company's enormous respect for Shakespeare; but it was also a way of turning the old plays, most of which were no longer current in the play-house, into ready money (the folio includes only Shake-speare's plays, not his sonnets or other nondramatic verse). Whatever the motives behind the publication of the folio, the texts it preserves constitute the basis for almost all later editions of the playwright's works. The texts, however, differ from those of the earlier quartos, sometimes in minor respects but often significantly – most strikingly in the two texts of *King Lear,* but also in important ways in *Hamlet, Othello,* and *Troilus and Cressida.* (The variants are recorded in the textual notes to each play in the new Pelican series.) The differences in these texts represent, in a sense, the essence of theater: the texts of plays were initially not intended for publication. They were scripts, designed for the actors to perform – the principal life of the play at this period was in performance. And it follows that in Shakespeare's theater the playwright typically had no say either in how his play was performed or in the disposition of his text – he was an employee of the company. The authoritative figures in the theatrical enterprise were the shareholders in the company, who were for the most part the major actors. They decided what plays were to be done; they hired the playwright and often gave him an outline of the play they wanted him to write. Often, too, the play was a collaboration: the company would retain a group of writers, and parcel out the scenes among them. The resulting script was then the property of the company, and the actors would revise it as they saw fit during the course of putting it on stage. The resulting text belonged to the company. The playwright had no rights in it once he had been paid. (This system survives largely intact in the movie industry, and most of the playwrights of Shakespeare's time were as anonymous as most screenwriters are today.) The script could also, of course, continue to change as the tastes of audiences and the requirements of the actors changed. Many – perhaps most – plays were revised when they were reintroduced after any substantial absence from the repertory, or when they were performed by a company different from the one that originally commissioned the play.

Shakespeare was an exceptional figure in this world because he was not only a shareholder and actor in his company, but also its leading playwright – he was literally his own boss. He had, moreover, little interest in the publication of his plays, and even those that appeared during his lifetime with the authorization of the company show no signs of any editorial concern on the part of the author. Theater was, for Shakespeare, a fluid and supremely responsive medium – the very opposite of the great classic canonical text that has embodied his works since 1623.

The very fluidity of the original texts, however, has meant that Shakespeare has always had to be edited. Here is an example of how problematic the editorial project inevitably is, a passage from the most famous speech in *Romeo and Juliet*, Juliet's balcony soliloquy beginning "O Romeo, Romeo, wherefore art thou Romeo?" Since the eighteenth century, the standard modern text has read,

> What's Montague? It is nor hand, nor foot,
> Nor arm, nor face, nor any other part
> Belonging to a man. O be some other name!
> What's in a name? That which we call a rose
> By any other name would smell as sweet.
>
> (II.2.40–44)

Editors have three early texts of this play to work from, two quarto texts and the folio. Here is how the First Quarto (1597) reads:

> Whats *Mountague?* It is nor hand nor foote,
> Nor arme, nor face, nor any other part.
> Whats in a name? That which we call a Rose,
> By any other name would smell as sweet:

Here is the Second Quarto (1599):

Whats *Mountague?* it is nor hand nor foote,
Nor arme nor face, ô be some other name
Belonging to a man.
Whats in a name that which we call a rose,
By any other word would smell as sweete,

And here is the First Folio (1623):

What's *Mountague?* it is nor hand nor foote,
Nor arme, nor face, O be some other name
Belonging to a man.
What? in a names that which we call a Rose,
By any other word would smell as sweete,

There is in fact no early text that reads as our modern text does – and this is the most famous speech in the play. Instead, we have three quite different texts, all of which are clearly some version of the same speech, but none of which seems to us a final or satisfactory version. The transcendently beautiful passage in modern editions is an editorial invention: editors have succeeded in conflating and revising the three versions into something we recognize as great poetry. Is this what Shakespeare "really" wrote? Who can say? What we can say is that Shakespeare always had performance, not a book, in mind.

Books About the Shakespeare Texts

The standard study of the printing history of the First Folio is W. W. Greg, *The Shakespeare First Folio* (1955). J. K. Walton, *The Quarto Copy for the First Folio of Shakespeare* (1971), is a useful survey of the relation of the quartos to the folio. The second edition of Charlton Hinman's *Norton Facsimile* of the First Folio (1996), with a new introduction by Peter Blayney, is indispensable. Stanley Wells and Gary Taylor, *William Shakespeare: A Textual Companion,* keyed to the Oxford text, gives a comprehensive survey of the editorial situation for all the plays and poems.

THE GENERAL EDITORS

Introduction

IN A MEMOIR entitled *Shakespearean Playgoing, 1890-1952* (London, 1953), Gordon Crosse wrote, "a really good performance of *Twelfth Night* is the perfection of pleasure that Shakespearean acting can give, at any rate in comedy." Much has changed in the second half of the twentieth century, including the staging and reception of Shakespeare's plays, yet Crosse's verdict would still be echoed by many theatergoers.

In what does this perfection consist? Although any answer must be speculative, the common testimony of readers and theatergoers would suggest that the play is singularly accessible and unthreatening; that its characters are generally engaging and its situations amusing; that its language is eloquent and sometimes magical; that its romantic intensity is rendered all the more appealing by Shakespeare's delicate irony; that its humor is "dry" (the play's own term) rather than harsh; that many of its characters, with the touchingly sorry exception of Sir Andrew Aguecheek, show a dazzling capacity for repartee; that the entertainment provided, by turns poignant and witty, sensitive and robust, verbal and musical, never palls; that its comic plots and motifs are skillfully integrated; that it is, generally speaking, a reader- and actor-friendly play. Paradoxically, the play's aristocratic settings and characters may, like those of *Love's Labors Lost,* add to its popular appeal; the real or imagined lives of the gentry make an ever-pleasing spectacle.

It would be easy, despite all the virtues of *Twelfth Night,* to question the play's "perfection" by drawing attention to recognized minor imperfections in the text or to unresolved tensions and numerous loose ends in the play. Indeed, it is difficult to overlook the darker, more disillusioning moments in *Twelfth Night* – among them, its ending with the melancholic clown, soaked to the skin, alone onstage – as well as the persistence in the play of cruel spectacle, such as the imprisonment of Malvolio, for which bearbaiting is one of the play's own recurrent metaphors. Yet the image of *Twelfth Night* as the perfect Shakespearean comedy persists, perhaps because many readers and audiences will have it so in keeping with the play's alternative title, *What You Will*.

Perhaps it is the same will, along with the play's aristocratic representations, that accounts for the persistence of a belief that *Twelfth Night* was written for private performance, or, according to Leslie Hotson in *The First Night of "Twelfth Night"* (London, 1954), for performance at the court of Queen Elizabeth I in 1601. (Twelfth Night, falling on January 6, was both a festive occasion and the date, twelve days after Christmas, on which the festive season traditionally ended.) Such views tend to imply that *Twelfth Night* is a play purged of the grossness of the Elizabethan public theater and intended for more "perfect" courtly settings. Hotson's ingenious speculations were fueled by the recorded visit of a Florentine count, Don Virginio Orsino, for whom the duke in the play may have been named, to the court in 1601. These speculations have now generally been found unconvincing, however, and their assumptions erroneous. The first recorded performance of the play took place in 1602, in the Middle Temple Hall belonging to the Inns of Court in London, where lawyers were trained. In other words, the setting was neither private nor particularly genteel. The attested success of the play in this and other historical settings does not necessarily imply its perfection, only its likeability. The fact that *Twelfth Night* is now a favorite for high-school reading and performance, for amateur and student theatricals, and as an introductory Shakespeare play similarly attests to its accessibility and ready appeal, not to any fastidious withdrawal of the play from the public domain. An impulse to withdraw is far more marked in such demanding or forbidding plays as *Hamlet, Troilus and Cressida,* and, above all, *Coriolanus.*

Both the public appeal and common substance of *Twelfth Night* derive in part from age-old European traditions of licensed festivity and exuberant "folly" that retained their power throughout the Middle Ages and up to Shakespeare's time. In ancient Rome, the term "Saturnalia" referred to forms of unrestrained merrymaking that marked the festival of Saturn, held in the middle of December, yet the term became more broadly synonymous with festivities in which public order, authority, and restraint were grossly flouted. The adjective "saturnalian" retains this sense in modern English. Obscene travesties were performed even, for example, in the wake of a Roman conqueror's triumphal entry into the city, as Shakespeare recalls in *Antony and Cleopatra.* Yet the Latin term *Saturnalia* also recalled the Age of Saturn as the legendary golden age of humankind before the advent of social inequality, war, poverty, labor, and oppression. To participate in the Saturnalia, as even slaves were licensed to do, was thus to commemorate a legendary better world and a common humanity; paradoxically, then, the most disorderly festivities partook of the sacred. Many Elizabethans never lost sight of the connection between "holiday" and "holy day," a perceived link that helps to account for the depth of contemporary resistance to Puritan attacks on the theaters and popular pastimes.

Saturnalian language and consciousness persisted strongly throughout the European Middle Ages, manifesting themselves in revelry, travesties and masquerades, aggressive verbal play, and celebrations of folly. The fool in *Twelfth Night* is appropriately named Feste, festivity incarnate. So-called Lords of Misrule, anticipating Shakespeare's Sir Toby Belch in *Twelfth Night* and Sir John Falstaff in the history plays, promoted festive disorderliness and bodily revolt against confining laws and manners; "I'll confine myself no finer than I am" (I.3.9), Sir Toby declares. When Sir Toby challenges Malvolio by saying

"Dost thou think, because thou art virtuous, there shall be no more cakes and ale?" (II.3.106), he speaks unanswerably for a saturnalian perspective on the world. Although the title *Twelfth Night* has no obvious relevance to the plot of Shakespeare's play, it is singularly appropriate to the revelry that infuses the play.

The fact that Malvolio tries to abridge the rights of festivity in *Twelfth Night* does, however, imply a historical conflict in Shakespeare's time between ancient saturnalian rites and the emergent power structures and civil disciplines of the post-Reformation world. In whatever way this conflict is explained – and the historical explanations are numerous – *Twelfth Night* reveals an underlying concern on Shakespeare's part with forms of historical untimeliness, upsetting grossness, incivility, excess, boredom, ill humor, cruelty, manipulation, irresponsibility, cynicism, and outright madness that had rendered festive culture questionable. Feste is a conspicuously melancholy, aging clown to whom Olivia remarks, "Now you see, sir, how your fooling grows old, and people dislike it" (I.5.106). The eloquently anti-festive Malvolio has found sympathizers among readers and theatergoers, and even the plotters against him in the play end up being uneasy about the cruel lengths to which they have gone. All these reservations – and the *qualified* praise of folly they dictate – do not suffice, however, to cancel *Twelfth Night*'s saturnalian heritage or negate the play's broad defense of festive pleasure. As a popular comedy of its time, *Twelfth Night* belongs inescapably to the world of folly. Consciousness of that setting pervades the play. The denial of folly and its pleasures, attempted by Malvolio in the play, can thus only seem like the greatest folly of all, whatever its reasons, and like the one intolerable form of foolishness. Referring to youthful pastimes and drunken revelries, even the great English Puritan author John Milton conceded in *Areopagitica*, "these things will be and must be." No longer finding these pleasures appealing rather than disapproving of them may indeed be one of the fears underlying the play's persistently expressed worries about aging.

What contributes as well as festivity to the relaxed atmosphere of *Twelfth Night* is the marked absence in the play of powerful authority figures, whether familial, political, or religious. The languages of all these forms of authority are parodied in *Twelfth Night,* and what the critic Marc Shell has called "universal siblinghood" tends to define the play's field of conflict, mischief, and tabooed "romance." Indeed, Shakespeare's revitalization of the conventional marriage plot of comedy in *Twelfth Night* depends on his redirection of incestuous sibling desire – "a brother's dead love," as Valentine ambiguously calls it (I.1.32) – into the socially approved channel of exogamous marriage. (Both this tabooed romance and its social redeployment are enacted in the wonderfully touching, ironic scene of Viola and Sebastian's reunion, arguably the single most romantic moment in the play.)

Although Duke Orsino outranks all others in this "sibling" domain, displaying self-centered willfulness of a kind that results in tragedy elsewhere in Shakespeare (when frustrated he speaks of wishing to kill the one he loves), he cannot impose his will on Olivia as the object of his courtship. The codes of romantic devotion, according to which the female beloved is to be worshiped, and must freely consent, restrain him. More important, Olivia's unusual independence as mistress of a household following the deaths of her father and brother (a situation no doubt modeled in part on that of the young Queen Elizabeth I) precludes Orsino from dominating her. In his comically languid, self-absorbed state as a lover, he displays little interest in exercising political power. Olivia's real freedom of choice is exercised when she chooses Sebastian.

As Olivia's uncle/kinsman, Sir Toby seeks to occupy the place of a father in her household, yet his unruly behavior makes him more like a wayward child or brother than a parent to her, and his calculating introduction of Sir An-

drew into her household as a suitor hardly fits him to be
her guardian. It is into the empty space of masculine authority, dignity, and control that Malvolio, Olivia's steward, also tries to insert himself, provoking brilliantly
inventive resistance. While *Twelfth Night* is a play more
realistic than utopian in the end, its festive freedom thus
apparently depends on a disabling of power and undoing
of normal structures of contemporary authority. In this
respect, the play offers both a relief from those tragically
fraught structures and a critical perspective on them. Yet
no final undoing of these structures is imagined in the
play. Utopianism and anti-utopianism aside, the play em-
bodies Shakespeare's consciousness that the old queen's
reign was drawing toward its end (she died in 1603) and
that an authoritarian male successor, James I, waited in
the wings. Although festivity would continue, and perhaps in grosser forms than those of the Elizabethan period, its implications would become less emancipatory.

The broad appeal of *Twelfth Night* as a good-humored,
festive play is sharpened and focused by its comedy of
mistaken identity. Although Viola and Sebastian are of
different sexes and cannot thus be biologically identical
twins, they cannot be distinguished from each other by
the other characters in the play when Viola disguises herself as a young man. In the hands of a skilled playwright,
the comedy of twins who are absurdly mistaken for each
other is practically fail-safe entertainment, as it is in
Twelfth Night. Both the comical predictability of the error
plot and the playwright's cleverness in wringing new sur-
prises out of it are a time-honored source of theatrical
delight. They have been so at least since the Roman playwright Plautus's *Menaechmi,* a direct ancestor of Shakespeare's *The Comedy of Errors* as well as *Twelfth Night.* In
the hands of a master of comedy like Plautus or Shakespeare, however, the changes rung on the comedy of
mistaken identity do not just result in hilarious cross-
purposes in the action – that is to say, in lively farce – but,
as many critics have noted, in a searching examination of

human identity in all its strangeness and paradoxicality. At their most abstract, the language and logic of identity in *Twelfth Night* go back as far as the philosophy of Aristotle, yet in the play that formal language and logic (parodied on occasion by the learned clown) are transposed into the medium of Elizabethan comedy. In *Twelfth Night,* Shakespeare partly recapitulates but also extends a humorous exploration of identity that he had begun in *The Comedy of Errors.*

Normally, we may infer from these plays, those who are not twins tend to take their identity for granted. The situation of identical twins, whose identities are forever at risk of being mistaken, seems anomalous. The peculiarity of an identical twin is that he or she is not unique (self-identical) but identical to someone else, thus apparently possessing only a shared, divided, or mirror identity. Such "double" identity is virtually a contradiction in terms, while repeatedly mistaken identity implies the lack of an unmistakable self. This peculiarity may help to explain why various cultures have regarded identical twins as unnatural or ominous, sometimes, indeed, to the point of killing them at birth. The supposed peculiarity of twins has also made their predicament a staple of comedy, as if they are a natural absurdity in a world where human dignity and even human status are virtually equated with the possession of unique identity.

Insofar as the comedy of mistaken identity exploits identical twins, making fun of their predicament, it implicitly upholds uniqueness as a social norm. Human society is tacitly being defined in such comedy as a community of individuals, the term "individual" meaning undivided or indivisible. Such a society will be one into which identical twins cannot smoothly be absorbed as doubles. Both the fear that twins are unnatural and the impulse to ridicule their plight survive in *Twelfth Night.* When Viola and Sebastian finally appear onstage together, thus putting an end to the mistakes of the play, both their naturalness and their divine wondrousness are affirmed to overcome any lingering, archaic fears that twins are unnatural or, in this case, a demonic illusion produced by artificial means (a so-called perspective glass):

> One face, one voice, one habit, and two persons –
> A natural perspective that is and is not.
>
> (V.1.211-12)

Both fear and the impulse to ridicule, then, without which there would be no comedy of mistaken identity, imply that twins represent a threat to an assumed norm of human identity. Yet in *Twelfth Night* the archaic cultural residue of twin anxiety seems limited – there is more of it in *The Comedy of Errors* – and the proclamation of Viola and Sebastian's wondrousness as twins accordingly seems both parodically excessive and teasingly romantic. (The "long-lost" routine through which Viola and Sebastian identify each other as siblings, and therefore non-marriageable, seems hardly necessary at the plot level, especially since Viola seems to have figured out by Act III that Sebastian is still alive, yet the taboo has to be re-marked.) Certainly in *Twelfth Night*, Shakespeare's twin characters are less an object of cultural dread than a complex theatrical device for plotting desire and identity in his own world.

Insofar as we are drawn into the twin characters' plight, we are pushed toward recognition that the singular identity we normally take for granted is also "mistaken." It is never absolute or self-sufficient, but exists only in a shared relation to others (or imaginary others), from whom it is derived or imitated. Parents, family members, lovers, friends, peers, colleagues, role models, social idols may all serve as alter egos. Not only do we learn our own vulnerability to nonrecognition and loss of dignity through our identification with stage twins, we are called on to recognize that the identity we carry around, as if it were a kind of inalienable property, exists only under particular conditions of place and time. The problems of twins in comedy generally begin when they move away from their usual place, and are suddenly mistaken or not recognized.

We also learn, still paradoxically, that individual identity depends on belonging to, and being recognized in, one or more social groups that may be signified by dress, manners, language, and a host of other defining traits. In the final act of *Twelfth Night,* Viola cannot be "herself" again until she changes back from men's clothing into women's – a return, however, that never takes place in the play. In short, the comedy of mistaken identity is a lesson in the complex, social, and always compromised nature of human identity. Even people's names, which are socially given, do not fully identify them in *Twelfth Night,* since they can be assumed, like "Cesario"; or shared, as we hear they were between Viola's father and brother, both called Sebastian; or resemble each other enough to make their bearers into oblique reflections and permutations of each other: for example, Olivia, Viola, Malvolio.

Of course, Shakespeare's *Twelfth Night* goes beyond mistaken identity as traditionally understood in comedy to include disguise and gender misrecognition, two definitive phenomena of the Elizabethan theater, in which women's parts were played by boy actors. To put it more strongly, the classic plot of mistaken identity, which depends on the biological phenomenon of same-sex identical twins, is rewritten in *Twelfth Night* to pose the question of *gendered* human identity and social performance. The twins in *Twelfth Night* are identical only when Viola is disguised as a young man, their apparent naturalness as identical twins thus being treated ironically. Here – and where is it not? – the "natural perspective" is a cultural product, not demonic deception but theatrical construction. Theoretically, it might have been possible for Shakespeare to have made the twins literally identical by using the same actor in both parts, but he calls for both to be onstage at the same time in Act V. He evidently wants them indistinguishable only to the characters, not to the audience, and the only thing that seems to make them identical is their clothing.

Viola's being mistaken for a young man results in something more than ordinary cross-purposes. In *The Comedy of Errors*, Shakespeare had already begun to complicate matters by introducing *two* pairs of male twins, one pair being freeborn and the other pair being born enslaved. Questions are implicitly posed in the play about whether identity belongs only to people of a certain class – those who own property – while being effectively denied to those who are owned. The slave twins are repeatedly beaten on being mistaken, and are thus physically marked as human property rather than as proprietors. They try to assert their own identity by outwitting their masters and resisting their impositions. In *Twelfth Night*, the question of who *has* identity is posed in the context of gender as well as property. Does full identity belong to men only, while such identity and dignity as women can enjoy must always be derived from men (fathers, brothers, lovers, husbands)? When Viola goes into male disguise, she assumes a male name and identity (Cesario), consciously stepping into the place of the brother (Sebastian) she believes has drowned. Is it only during an interlude of "playing the man," whether in male disguise like Viola or as an independent property owner before marriage like Olivia, that women can temporarily borrow "real" identity from men? The postponement of Viola's return to her feminine self in *Twelfth Night* prompts us to consider what she has to lose rather than gain by ceasing to be Cesario, and becoming Orsino's wife. When the actress Joan Plowright played both twin parts in a 1970 ATV production of *Twelfth Night*, she challenged the implicit masculine exclusiveness of identity as well as the Shakespearean stage actuality of an all-male cast. Some more recent performances of the play, implicitly questioning the "human" identity of those onstage, include ones using puppets or animation.

Twelfth Night additionally prompts us to inquire how, if identity is a function of gender, men and women deal with their own consciousness of being divided between impulses socially coded as exclusively male or exclusively female. How do they come to terms with selves that are not only internally divided but internally questing, fluid, and even promiscuous, their wishes not necessarily capable of being played out in any single identity, role, or gender? The "androgynous" Viola, unsettled in desire herself despite her having fixed on Orsino as the most eligible bachelor around, and desirable to both men and women, precipitates just such issues in the play. As Cesario, she becomes a disorienting object of attraction to both a man and a woman. Orsino responds to her with considerable erotic intensity in her guise as a young man, but also bonds with her as a male confidant despite her feminine traits; in both these respects, Orsino is unconsciously and perhaps dangerously deviating from social norms. Olivia responds to Viola with excitement but also with distress, since it is improper for her to court Orsino's messenger; improper for her to take the active role, especially with a male subordinate; and perhaps (unconsciously) improper to court one of such feminine appearance. Viola thus deflects conventional heterosexual courtship in the play, disrupting its normalized hierarchies and trajectories. Despite her expanded field of action in male disguise, she also finds herself painfully divided, thwarted, and threatened with disablement in the world of conventional courtly romance, in which Orsino plays his part as lover by the book. Conveying her own predicament to Orsino as if it were that of a dead sister (an imaginary twin), she says her sister could not "[tell] her love" (II.4.110). In other words, Viola is saying that *she* cannot tell Orsino that she loves him, and is therefore silent even in the act of conversing with him. Yet she also articulates the broader difficulty of ever avowing one's love fully or knowing its true object: there is always more than can be told, or something that cannot be told, whatever the circumstances.

The fact that things never fully return to "normal" in

the play after this androgynous interlude, not even when identities and genders have been sorted out and the marriage of the favored principals is anticipated, indicates that socially mandated heterosexual marriage cannot resolve all issues of desire and identity, restoring everyone to his or her supposedly proper self. On the contrary, what the psychoanalytic critic Jacqueline Rose has written about Sigmund Freud's attempt to organize human identities and relations applies to Shakespeare's *Twelfth Night* as well:

> Order [also means] sexual order, the division of human subjects into male and female and the directing of desire on to its appropriate objects, but . . . this is effected only partially and at a cost. ("Sexuality in the Reading of Shakespeare: *Hamlet* and *Measure for Measure*," in *Alternative Shakespeares*, ed. John Drakakis [Methuen, 1985]: 99)

Shakespeare, like Freud, values order (or finds it inescapable), balancing its benefits against its costs in repression and social exclusion of the nonconforming. Yet to state the issue only in these cost-benefit terms is misleading in Shakespeare's case. In *Twelfth Night*, androgyny, transvestism, and same-sex pursuit (the male version of which, represented in the play by Antonio and Sebastian, was known to Elizabethans as "masculine love") can seem like rich, imaginative alternatives to passively received codes of heterosexual courtship and simple male-female identification. In a manner consistent with the play's alternative title, *What You Will*, identities and roles can be doubled, improvised, or transgressively played, both despite and because of coercive, homogenizing social norms.

The particular conditions of the Elizabethan English theater from which *Twelfth Night* emerged are partly responsible for the play's continuing appeal and its compelling exploration of desire, gender, and identity. Elizabethan entertainment relied heavily on the elements of disguise, deception, and multiple role-playing exploited by Shakespeare in *Twelfth Night,* thus inevitably prompting playwrights to question any simple view of human identity. The use of boy actors in women's parts similarly provoked searching reflection on human desire and gender performance, neither of which seems simple or biologically predetermined. The durable appeal of *Twelfth Night,* among other plays by Shakespeare and his contemporaries, owes much to the imaginative questioning pursued in the Elizabethan theater as a microcosm of the larger contemporary world.

Cultural anxieties acted out in the Elizabethan theater have never been wholly defused; indeed, the resurgence of similar anxieties has been a marked phenomenon of our time. Fears regarding the security and integrity of the self were almost inevitably provoked in the Elizabethan theatrical world of endless performance, masquerade, and artful illusion. Contemporary English Puritans invoked biblical and philosophical tradition (Saint Paul as well as Plato) in denouncing the theater as a place of false appearances and idolatrous images. Similarly, the contemporary Puritans quoted prohibitions on cross-dressing in Leviticus when attacking the stage, and frequently denounced onstage courtships involving men and cross-dressing boy actors as sodomitical in themselves and incitements to sodomy in others. Yet the virulence of the Puritan attack on the theaters does not mean that Puritans were immune to the power of Elizabethan plays: on the contrary, these attacks reveal a horrified fascination with the theater of the time.

A powerful wish to sort out truth from appearances, nature from culture, and identity from doubleness is certainly played out to some effect in the clarification scene (*anagnorisis*) in *Twelfth Night,* when both twins are finally present together onstage. This process remains teasingly incomplete or confusing, however, since Viola never reappears in her woman's costume (in the story, it has been

stored at the inn by the sea captain, who alone can re-
trieve it). Who or what is s/he, then, in this forever sus-
pended moment? Boy, girl, or boy-girl? Female character
in disguise or boy-actor undisguised? Where does the
truth lie, in fiction or in fact? In nature or culture? Onstage or offstage? How secure are the boundaries between
any of these realms? Since the meaning of "natural" slides
between "according to nature" and "idiotic" throughout
the play, as it does in Elizabethan English generally, what
it would mean to return to nature is never fully determined, nor is any such return necessarily to be desired.
And, despite hints that something momentous will be revealed in *Twelfth Night*, no divine revelation of the true
order of things is forthcoming.

It is not the drama of desire crisscrossing with gendered
identity alone, however, that accounts for the continuing
appeal of *Twelfth Night*. The play caters variously to its
audiences, offering broad comedy, poignant romance,
and sardonic observation (the latter primarily from the
fool) in typically mixed Shakespearean fashion. The plot
of intrigue in the play draws on the conventions of popular "gulling" comedy. In this plot, the calculating Sir Toby,
not quite the jolly roisterer he seems, aims to dupe foolish
Sir Andrew (the "gull") out of his money. When Malvolio
rebukes Sir Toby and his rowdy drinking companions for
disturbing the peace of Olivia's household, however, Sir
Toby's accomplice and eventual wife, Maria, takes over
the plotting and makes Malvolio the object of her gulling
ingenuity. He then becomes the victim in a cruelly effective plot of public humiliation.

The neatly interlocking plots of the play – of mistaken
identity and of Malvolio's exposure to ridicule – were ap-
preciatively noted by the law student John Manningham
in his oft-quoted diary entry regarding the 1602 performance of *Twelfth Night*:

> At our feast we had a play called *Twelfth Night, or
> What You Will*, much like *The Comedy of Errors* or

> *Menaechmi* in Plautus . . . a good practice in it to
> make the steward believe his lady widow was in love
> with him by counterfeiting a letter as from his
> lady . . . and then when he came to practise, making
> him believe they took him to be mad. (Cited in S.
> Schoenbaum, *William Shakespeare: A Documentary
> Life* [Oxford, 1975]: 156)

Both the familiarity and the "good practice" (that is, good
trick) of the plotting in *Twelfth Night* go a long way toward explaining its staying power: even now, its conventions and materials are not unrecognizable by theater
audiences. (On the Internet, films of *Twelfth Night* evidently present no problems of classification, the readily
applied key words being Romance, Comedy, Drama.) In-
terestingly, however, Manningham misremembers Olivia
as a widow. The theatrical and cultural stereotype to
which he is assimilating the Malvolio plot is one of marriage to a rich widow. Such was the scenario in the play's
source, Barnabe Rich's *A Farewell to the Military Profes-
sion,* yet Shakespeare changed it in *Twelfth Night.* A
closely related scenario, more anxiety-provoking and less
stereotypically bourgeois, appears to be operative in
Shakespeare's Malvolio plot. By the same token, the problem presented by Malvolio in the play is more complex
than first impressions would suggest.

It is easy to see the threat Malvolio presents as "a kind
of Puritan" to the members of Olivia's household as well
as to the festive world of the play. In effect, he is the nega-
tion of practically everything that makes *Twelfth Night* the
delight it is, and must therefore be overcome. Audiences
generally want to see Malvolio defeated, much as contemporary TV audiences want to see the Grinch who stole
Christmas defeated. Yet the clarity with which the battle
lines are drawn and the ease of the plotters' victory over
Malvolio are perhaps a little too satisfying. There is more
to Malvolio than a wish to banish cakes and ale. He will
neither be forgotten nor relinquish his legal rights, and no

one in the play can overbear him. Indeed, in a breathtaking surprise twist right at the end of the play, it appears that the sea captain, who has stored Viola's clothes, is imprisoned "at Malvolio's suit" (V.1.271). Malvolio must therefore be brought back into the play just when everyone has happily forgotten him. "Suit" also turns out to refer not only to stage clothing but to lawsuits, and Malvolio turns out to have one more suit than anyone, onstage or off, has bargained for. When summoned, Malvolio leaves again swearing revenge rather than accepting reconciliation, and technically holds the happy ending of the play hostage. Even Orsino apparently cannot impose his will, saying "Pursue him and entreat him to a peace. / He hath not told us of the captain yet" (V.1.373-74). We will never hear this story or know the outcome, a state of suspense that leaves Malvolio with a mysterious hold over the play. In fact, it is far from clear that Malvolio *can* be mollified and that the story *can* have a happy ending; for Viola to marry Orsino would seem to require a whole new play, with Malvolio at its center.

What problem does Malvolio pose, then? Recent critics have noted that the plotters in the play take exception, not just to Malvolio's repressiveness, but to his aspiration toward upward social mobility. This aspiration does not mean that Malvolio is an intrusive "lower-class" character – there are no such characters in *Twelfth Night* – but it does mean that Malvolio is seen as having inappropriate aspirations. Sir Toby tries to put him in his place: "Art any more than a steward?" (II.3.105-6). The plot against Malvolio, devised by Maria, at once triggers and exposes his almost explicitly masturbatory fantasy of wedding Olivia, his employer, and taking control of her household. In Malvolio's fantasy, his own sexual gratification in Olivia's bed will coincide with his social gratification as master both of her and her household. He imagines – thus scandalizing as well as threatening other members of the household – that desire (Olivia's for him) will dissolve the barriers separating them.

What makes Malvolio so disturbing a figure is that in the gentlemanly world of *Twelfth Night,* and, by implication, of Elizabethan England, issues of status and legitimate aspiration remain significantly unresolved. Orsino may outrank all others in the play, just as Olivia outranks Malvolio as his employer, yet status in the play isn't decisively signaled by differences of language, trade, or manners. (Sir Toby isn't marrying down, for example, when he chooses Maria, an upper servant not risen from the peasantry, nor is he losing status when he engages in drunken revelry and swearing.) Limits to the entitlement and mobility of characters belonging to that world remain sufficiently undefined to cause anxiety, as does the question of who properly belongs to the sphere of gentility. Neither in *Twelfth Night* nor in Elizabethan England does that sphere include only those who are, as Malvolio says, "born great": it is a sphere of broadly genteel origins, literacy, and acquired good manners, open to many.

Although Malvolio may be mad to dream of a dramatic change in his fortunes within that sphere, he is not alone in dreaming of it. Elizabethan romance stories had implanted in more minds than Malvolio's the belief that in a world governed by fortune such changes were possible. The same romances had taught that crisscrossing desires could breach status barriers, giving subordinates access to higher status and greater sexual freedom. (Malvolio dreams of having sex in the daytime, an aristocratic luxury.) The "mad" presumptuousness of fantasies like Malvolio's meant, however, that their exposure was mortifying in the highest degree, as the exposure of Malvolio's "shameful" fantasy is to him. Theater audiences may feel embarrassed *for* him as well as laugh at him.

It is because Malvolio's dream is a common dream, not some unspeakable private fantasy, that Maria can set an effective trap. She need only exploit her knowledge of Malvolio and her social intuition to succeed. The means she uses to trap Malvolio are keyed to norms of the time. She drops a forged letter for Malvolio to find that will seem to him like an obliquely worded love letter from Olivia. In a constrained, decorous society, one important way of communicating forbidden desires was through insinuating, secret letters. The fact that the forged letter *is* cryptic incites Malvolio to decode it and also convinces him that it is an authentic love letter from Olivia. In the culture represented by *Twelfth Night*, a clear declaration by Olivia would be implausible.

Insinuating letters often circulate in romance stories of the time, yet historical evidence shows that they also circulated in fact in the somewhat promiscuous, politically conniving court societies of Renaissance Europe. Both Maria's ploy and Malvolio's falling for it reveal how codified these particular romance fantasies and practices were in Shakespeare's world. Nevertheless, a line is drawn at Malvolio's aspirations. Or, to put it differently, the extravagance of Malvolio's implanted aspirations allows a line to be drawn in, and perhaps beyond, the play. The humiliation of Malvolio in the play could hardly have failed to operate as a public warning as well: know your place; do not presume too far; do not take the promises of romance too seriously; do not take fiction literally. That admonition would have held even if, as Malvolio says, "There is example for't" (II.5.36) – that is, real life contains examples of such abrupt changes of fortune. To the extent that Malvolio's fate serves as a warning, Maria's play-within-the-play is performing one of the main traditional functions of comedy – namely, to impose discipline and inflict punishment on social transgressors.

Contrary to first impressions, it is the repressive, controlling, yet *desiring* Malvolio – not the riotous Sir Toby – who is potentially the most disruptive figure in *Twelfth Night:* generally disruptive to status regulation, and particularly disruptive of the "gentle" romance world of the self-affirming, well-born characters in the play. While romantic passion is feared as a form of madness by various characters in *Twelfth Night*, Malvolio's madness alone is singled out for punishment, not reward. Led on by

Maria's forgery, he allows himself to take the promises of romance too literally as he pores over individual letters in the forged letter to make them into an anagram of his name. His literal reading of the letter – his scouring of it for every possible clue – is represented as being foreign to the gentle spirit of romance. As a way of reading, it is wholly self-centered, it is humorless, it is forced, it greedily sexualizes the body of the woman who is imagined to have written it. Indeed, Malvolio's breaking of Olivia's seal on the letter, on which a picture of the chaste Lucrece is imprinted, is fully analogized to rape.

Through the exposure of Malvolio – but of a strangely provocative Olivia, too? – in this scene of bad reading, the play suggests what does not belong to ideal gentility, hence to *Twelfth Night*. Power seeking, arrogant authority, self-centeredness, violence, sexual explicitness, forced interpretation are all to be excluded – but so, it would seem, are people who don't really belong anyway. The plot that exposes Malvolio is also an outing of the outsider, the "hidden" threat he represents in the gentle world thus being exposed (a strategy that threatens to backfire, of course, if, as an outsider with the law on his side, Malvolio cannot be brought back in again and reconciled).

Paradoxically, it is Malvolio's excess of desire rather than any lack of it that makes him seem dangerous. He may feel uncomfortable when, deceived by the letter, he appears before Olivia cross-gartered, wearing yellow stockings, and smiling continuously (thus making a pitiful fool of himself), yet this new costume also reveals an extravagant Malvolio belied by his habitual sobriety in office as a steward. It is at such wild extravagance and drastic metamorphosis that the play apparently balks, partly in its own defense, and partly in defense of its ideally gentle world.

As much as Malvolio is an agent of repression in the play, he is ultimately the object of its repression. Shakespeare's humorously tolerant and generally expansive treatment of identity in *Twelfth Night* has its repressive, scathing counterpart in the treatment of Malvolio. If

Malvolio remains a somewhat haunting figure, it is perhaps chiefly for that reason, but also because he stands for some common human realities (being at a social disadvantage, being literal, being greedy, being gullible, being self-centered) that are not only disowned in the play but subjected to overkill. Although Maria is the author of the letter that deceives Malvolio, his reading it aloud makes *him* primarily responsible for that letter's humorously deidealizing reminder of the private parts and bodily functions the idealized Olivia shares with ordinary mortals. Malvolio cannot be exposed, in other words, without some of the limits and conditions of gentle Shakespearean comedy being exposed as well.

For John Manningham in 1602, *Twelfth Night* evidently provoked no second thoughts. For us it may do so. In any event, the play's alternative title, *What You Will,* transfers responsibility for the play to successive readers and theater audiences, without whose collaboration it would perish in any case. Resistance to this transfer of responsibility as well as a desire to keep the pleasures of *Twelfth Night* pure and simple is revealed by those editors and critics who insist that as a title "what you will" means no more than "call it what you like." Yet the meaning of the alternative title cannot be arbitrarily restricted in this way, and the attempt is only self-betraying. For better or worse, the play lends itself both to social reflection and self-reflection. Refusal of this task is certainly compatible with the spirited defense of pleasure in the play, yet it amounts to a refusal to read the play to its fullest effect — or to be read by it. In this respect, what "you" will remains both a collective and an individual choice.

JONATHAN CREWE
Dartmouth College

Note on the Text

TWELFTH NIGHT was first printed in the 1623 folio edition of Shakespeare's plays. The folio text is relatively error free, and some errors that did find their way into the first folio were corrected in the second folio, of 1632. Succeeding editors subsequently corrected obvious mistakes and inconsistencies still missed in the second folio, yet the initially "clean" folio text has made editing this play relatively unproblematic and noncontroversial. In this edition, I have made relatively few departures from the previously established Pelican Shakespeare text, and have kept most of the glosses.

Following is a complete list of substantive departures from the folio text, with the adopted reading in italics followed by the folio reading in roman.

I.2 15 *Arion* Orion
I.3 48 *Andrew* Ma. 52 *Mary Accost* Mary, accost 57 *Fare* Far 86 *Pourquoi* Pur-quoy 87 *pourquoi* purquoy 93 *curl by* coole my 95 *me* we 97 *housewife* huswife 119 *Mall's* Mals 127 *dun* dam'd; *set* sit 130 *That's* That
I.4 28 *nuncio's* Nuntio's
I.5 110 *comes* – comes 142 *Has* Ha's 160 s.d. *Viola* Violenta 164 *beauty* – beautie. 202 *olive* Olyffe
II.2 12 *me.* me – 31 *our* O 32 *made of, such* made, if such
II.3 2 *diluculo* Deliculo 24 *leman* Lemon 32 *a* – a 125 *a nayword* an ayword
II.4 53 *Fly . . . fly* fye . . . fie 88 *I* It 99 *suffers* suffer
II.5 57 *my* – *some* my some 109 *staniel* stallion 124 *sequel. That* sequell that 137 *born* become; *achieve* atcheeues 151–52 *Unhappy." Daylight* unhappy daylight 168 *dear* deero
III.1 8 *king lies* King s lyes 67 *wise men, folly-fall'n* wisemens folly falne 70 *vous garde* vou garde 71 *vous aussi; votre* vouz ousie vostre 90 *all ready* already
III.2 7 *thee the* the
III.4 22 *Olivia* Mal. 66 *tang* langer 158 *Fare thee well* Fartheewell 165 *You* Yon 236 *competent* Computent 247 s.d. *Exit* Exit Toby 340 *babbling, drunkenness* babling drunkennesse 379 s.d. *Exeunt* Exit
IV.2 5 *in* in in 37 *clerestories* cleere stores 69 *sport to* sport
V.1 115 *thief* thief 195 *pavin* panym 201 *help? An* help an 343 *mad. Thou cam'st* mad; then cam'st 387, 391, 395, 399 *the wind . . . rain* &c. 389, 393, 397 *it . . . day* &c. 399 *With hey* hey

Twelfth Night

or

What You Will

Twelfth Night

or

What You Will

◈ I.1 *Enter Orsino Duke of Illyria, Curio, and other Lords [with Musicians].*

DUKE
If music be the food of love, play on,
Give me excess of it, that, surfeiting,
The appetite may sicken, and so die.
That strain again, it had a dying fall;   4
O, it came o'er my ear like the sweet sound
That breathes upon a bank of violets,
Stealing and giving odor. Enough, no more;
'Tis not so sweet now as it was before.
O spirit of love, how quick and fresh art thou,   9
That notwithstanding thy capacity   *10*
Receiveth as the sea, naught enters there,
Of what validity and pitch soe'er,   *12*
But falls into abatement and low price
Even in a minute. So full of shapes is fancy   *14*
That it alone is high fantastical.   *15*

I.1 The palace of Duke Orsino   **4** *fall* cadence   **9** *quick* alive   **12** *validity* value; *pitch* i.e., worth (in falconry, high point of a falcon's flight)   **14** *shapes* imagined forms; *fancy* love   **15** *high fantastical* highly imaginative, extravagant

CURIO
　Will you go hunt, my lord?

DUKE
　What, Curio?

CURIO
　The hart.

DUKE
　Why, so I do, the noblest that I have.
20　O, when mine eyes did see Olivia first,
　Methought she purged the air of pestilence.
22　That instant was I turned into a hart,
23　And my desires, like fell and cruel hounds,
　E'er since pursue me.
　　　　　Enter Valentine.
　　　　　　　　　How now? What news from her?

VALENTINE
　So please my lord, I might not be admitted,
　But from her handmaid do return this answer:
27　The element itself, till seven years' heat,
　Shall not behold her face at ample view;
29　But like a cloistress she will veilèd walk,
30　And water once a day her chamber round
31　With eye-offending brine: all this to season
　A brother's dead love, which she would keep fresh
　And lasting in her sad remembrance.

DUKE
　O, she that hath a heart of that fine frame
　To pay this debt of love but to a brother,
36　How will she love when the rich golden shaft
　Hath killed the flock of all affections else
　That live in her; when liver, brain, and heart,
　These sovereign thrones, are all supplied and filled,
40　Her sweet perfections, with one self king.

22–24 *hart . . . me* (alluding to Ovid's story of Actaeon, turned into a hart by
Diana and killed by his own hounds) 23 *fell* savage 27 *element* sky; *heat*
course 29 *cloistress* nun 31 *brine* tears; *season* preserve 36–37 *when . . .*
else i.e., when Cupid's arrow has slain all emotions except love

Away before me to sweet beds of flow'rs;
Love thoughts lie rich when canopied with bow'rs.

Exeunt.

*

∾ **I.2** *Enter Viola, a Captain, and Sailors.*

VIOLA
  What country, friends, is this?
CAPTAIN
  This is Illyria, lady.   2
VIOLA
  And what should I do in Illyria?
  My brother he is in Elysium.   4
  Perchance he is not drowned. What think you, sailors?
CAPTAIN
  It is perchance that you yourself were saved.
VIOLA
  O my poor brother, and so perchance may he be.
CAPTAIN
  True, madam; and, to comfort you with chance,   8
  Assure yourself, after our ship did split,
  When you, and those poor number saved with you,   *10*
  Hung on our driving boat, I saw your brother,   11
  Most provident in peril, bind himself
  (Courage and hope both teaching him the practice)
  To a strong mast that lived upon the sea;   14
  Where, like Arion on the dolphin's back,   15
  I saw him hold acquaintance with the waves
  So long as I could see.
VIOLA
  For saying so, there's gold.

I.2 The seacoast of Illyria **2** *Illyria* on the east coast of the Adriatic **4** *Elysium* home of the blessed dead **8** *chance* what may have happened **11** *driving* drifting **14** *lived* floated **15** *Arion* a Greek bard who leapt overboard to escape murderous sailors, and charmed dolphins with the music of his lyre so that they bore him to land

19   Mine own escape unfoldeth to my hope,
20   Whereto thy speech serves for authority
      The like of him. Know'st thou this country?

CAPTAIN
      Ay, madam, well, for I was bred and born
      Not three hours' travel from this very place.

VIOLA
      Who governs here?

CAPTAIN
      A noble duke, in nature as in name.

VIOLA
      What is his name?

CAPTAIN
      Orsino.

VIOLA
      Orsino! I have heard my father name him.
      He was a bachelor then.

CAPTAIN
30   And so is now, or was so very late;
      For but a month ago I went from hence,
32   And then 'twas fresh in murmur (as you know
      What great ones do, the less will prattle of)
      That he did seek the love of fair Olivia.

VIOLA
      What's she?

CAPTAIN
      A virtuous maid, the daughter of a count
      That died some twelvemonth since, then leaving her
      In the protection of his son, her brother,
      Who shortly also died; for whose dear love,
40   They say, she hath abjured the sight
      And company of men.

VIOLA   O that I served that lady,
42   And might not be delivered to the world,

_____
19 *unfoldeth to my hope* gives me hope (for my brother)   32 *fresh in murmur*
a current rumor   40 *abjured* renounced   42 *delivered* revealed

Till I had made mine own occasion mellow,   43
What my estate is.   44
CAPTAIN   That were hard to compass,
Because she will admit no kind of suit,
No, not the duke's.
VIOLA
There is a fair behavior in thee, captain,   47
And though that nature with a beauteous wall
Doth oft close in pollution, yet of thee   49
I will believe thou hast a mind that suits   50
With this thy fair and outward character.   51
I prithee (and I'll pay thee bounteously)
Conceal me what I am, and be my aid
For such disguise as haply shall become   54
The form of my intent. I'll serve this duke.   55
Thou shalt present me as an eunuch to him;   56
It may be worth thy pains. For I can sing
And speak to him in many sorts of music
That will allow me very worth his service.   59
What else may hap, to time I will commit;   60
Only shape thou thy silence to my wit.
CAPTAIN
Be you his eunuch, and your mute I'll be;   62
When my tongue blabs, then let mine eyes not see.
VIOLA
I thank thee. Lead me on.   *Exeunt.*

                              *

---

43 *mellow* ready to be revealed   **44** *estate* position in society; *compass* bring about   **47** *behavior* both "conduct" and "appearance"   **49** *pollution* corruption   **51** *character* personal appearance indicating moral qualities   **54** *haply* by chance   **55** *form of my intent* my outward purpose   **56** *eunuch* castrato, or young male singer, emasculated to preserve his high voice   **59** *allow me* cause me to be considered   **62** *mute* silent attendant

‿ **I.3** *Enter Sir Toby and Maria.*

TOBY   What a plague means my niece to take the death
    of her brother thus? I am sure care's an enemy to life.

MARIA   By my troth, Sir Toby, you must come in earlier
4   o' nights. Your cousin, my lady, takes great exceptions
    to your ill hours.

6 TOBY   Why, let her except before excepted.

MARIA   Ay, but you must confine yourself within the
    modest limits of order.

9 TOBY   Confine? I'll confine myself no finer than I am.
10   These clothes are good enough to drink in, and so be
11   these boots too. An they be not, let them hang them-
    selves in their own straps.

MARIA   That quaffing and drinking will undo you. I
    heard my lady talk of it yesterday; and of a foolish
    knight that you brought in one night here to be her
    wooer.

TOBY   Who? Sir Andrew Aguecheek?

MARIA   Ay, he.

19 TOBY   He's as tall a man as any's in Illyria.

20 MARIA   What's that to th' purpose?

21 TOBY   Why, he has three thousand ducats a year.

MARIA   Ay, but he'll have but a year in all these ducats.
    He's a very fool and a prodigal.

24 TOBY   Fie that you'll say so! He plays o' th' viol-de-
    gamboys, and speaks three or four languages word for
26   word without book, and hath all the good gifts of nature.

27 MARIA   He hath, indeed, almost natural; for, besides that
    he's a fool, he's a great quarreler; and but that he hath
29   the gift of a coward to allay the gust he hath in quarrel-

---

I.3 The house of Countess Olivia   **4** *cousin* kinsman   **6** *except before ex-*
cepted (cant legal phrase)   **9** *finer* both "tighter" and "better"   **11** *An* if   **19**
tall both "tall" and "brave"   **21** *ducats* Venetian gold coins   **24–25** *viol-de-*
gamboys "leg-viola," predecessor of the violoncello   **26** *without book* by
memory   **27** *natural* i.e., as a fool   **29** *gust* taste

ing, 'tis thought among the prudent he would quickly   *30*
have the gift of a grave.

TOBY   By this hand, they are scoundrels and substractors   *32*
that say so of him. Who are they?

MARIA   They that add, moreover, he's drunk nightly in
your company.

TOBY   With drinking healths to my niece. I'll drink to
her as long as there is a passage in my throat and drink
in Illyria. He's a coward and a coistrel that will not   *38*
drink to my niece till his brains turn o' th' toe like a
parish top. What, wench? *Castiliano vulgo;* for here   *40*
comes Sir Andrew Agueface.   *41*

    Enter Sir Andrew.

ANDREW   Sir Toby Belch. How now, Sir Toby Belch?

TOBY   Sweet Sir Andrew.

ANDREW   Bless you, fair shrew.

MARIA   And you too, sir.

TOBY   Accost, Sir Andrew, accost.   *46*

ANDREW   What's that?

TOBY   My niece's chambermaid.

ANDREW   Good Mistress Accost, I desire better acquaintance.   *50*

MARIA   My name is Mary, sir.

ANDREW   Good Mistress Mary Accost –

TOBY   You mistake, knight. "Accost" is front her, board   *53*
her, woo her, assail her.

ANDREW   By my troth, I would not undertake her in this   *55*
company. Is that the meaning of "accost"?

MARIA   Fare you well, gentlemen.

TOBY   An thou let part so, Sir Andrew, would thou
mightst never draw sword again.

---

32 *substractors* detractors   **38** *coistrel* horse groom, base fellow   **40** *parish top*
large top used for public amusement; *Castiliano vulgo* (of doubtful meaning;
Castilians were noted for decorum, and this may be a plea for "common po-
liteness")   **41** *Agueface* pale and thin-faced, like a man suffering from the
acute fever of ague   **46** *Accost* make up to (her)   **53** *front* face; *board* greet
(literally, go on board, but here with sexual innuendo)   **55** *undertake* take
on, with sexual implication of "take below"

60 ANDREW An you part so, mistress, I would I might never
    draw sword again! Fair lady, do you think you have
    fools in hand?

MARIA Sir, I have not you by th' hand.

64 ANDREW Marry, but you shall have, and here's my hand.

MARIA Now, sir, thought is free. I pray you, bring your
66 hand to th' butt'ry bar and let it drink.

ANDREW Wherefore, sweetheart? What's your meta-
    phor?

69 MARIA It's dry, sir.

70 ANDREW Why, I think so. I am not such an ass but I can
    keep my hand dry. But what's your jest?

MARIA A dry jest, sir.

ANDREW Are you full of them?

MARIA Ay, sir, I have them at my fingers' ends. Marry,
75 now I let go your hand, I am barren.   *Exit.*

76 TOBY O knight, thou lack'st a cup of canary! When did I
77 see thee so put down?

ANDREW Never in your life, I think, unless you see ca-
    nary put me down. Methinks sometimes I have no
80 more wit than a Christian or an ordinary man has. But
    I am a great eater of beef, and I believe that does harm
    to my wit.

TOBY No question.

ANDREW An I thought that, I'd forswear it. I'll ride
    home tomorrow, Sir Toby.

86 TOBY *Pourquoi,* my dear knight?

ANDREW What is *"pourquoi"*? Do, or not do? I would I
88 had bestowed that time in the tongues that I have in

---

64 *Marry* indeed, to be sure (originally an oath on the name of the Virgin
Mary) **66** *butt'ry bar* storeroom, from the bar of which liquor and provi-
sions were served; here, too, Maria's breasts; *it* i.e., your hand **69** *dry* both
"old" and "dryly humorous" **70–71** *I am . . . dry* fools proverbially knew
how to stay dry **75** *barren* i.e., barren of jokes **76** *canary* a sweet wine
from the Canary Islands **77** *put down* discomfited **80** *Christian* i.e., humble, but perhaps humorless, too **86** *Pourquoi* why **88** *tongues* languages,
perhaps with a pun on "tongs," curling irons

fencing, dancing, and bearbaiting. O, had I but fol- 89
lowed the arts! 90

TOBY   Then hadst thou had an excellent head of hair.

ANDREW   Why, would that have mended my hair? 92

TOBY   Past question, for thou seest it will not curl by nature.

ANDREW   But it becomes me well enough, does't not?

TOBY   Excellent. It hangs like flax on a distaff; and I hope 96
to see a housewife take thee between her legs and spin it 97
off.

ANDREW   Faith, I'll home tomorrow, Sir Toby. Your
niece will not be seen; or if she be, it's four to one she'll 100
none of me. The count himself here hard by woos her.

TOBY   She'll none o' th' count. She'll not match above
her degree, neither in estate, years, nor wit; I have heard 103
her swear't. Tut, there's life in't, man.

ANDREW   I'll stay a month longer. I am a fellow o' th'
strangest mind i' th' world. I delight in masques and 106
revels sometimes altogether. 107

TOBY   Art thou good at these kickshawses, knight? 108

ANDREW   As any man in Illyria, whatsoever he be, under
the degree of my betters, and yet I will not compare 110
with an old man. 111

TOBY   What is thy excellence in a galliard, knight? 112

ANDREW   Faith, I can cut a caper. 113

TOBY   And I can cut the mutton to't. 114

---

89 *bearbaiting* popular spectacle in which a tied bear was tormented by dogs
90 *arts* liberal arts such as languages   **92** *mended* improved   **96** *flax on a
distaff* straight strings of flax, spun on a stick held between the spinning-
woman's legs   **97–98** *spin it off* lose hair as a result of venereal disease   **103**
degree rank in society; *estate* fortune; *wit* intelligence   **106–7** *masques and
revels* court entertainments, involving masquerade, performance, and dancing   **107** *altogether* in all respects   **108** *kickshawses* trifles (French *quelque
chose*)   **111** *old man* probably "experienced person"   **112** *galliard* quick
dance in triple time   **113** *caper* frolicsome leap; also a spice used with mutton   **114** *cut the mutton* i.e., the mutton served with capers, but also implying sex with a prostitute ("mutton," in Elizabethan slang)

115 ANDREW And I think I have the back-trick simply as
    strong as any man in Illyria.

    TOBY Wherefore are these things hid? Wherefore have
118   these gifts a curtain before 'em? Are they like to take
119   dust, like Mistress Mall's picture? Why dost thou not
120   go to church in a galliard and come home in a coranto?
    My very walk should be a jig. I would not so much
122   as make water but in a sink-a-pace. What dost thou
    mean? Is it a world to hide virtues in? I did think, by
    the excellent constitution of thy leg, it was formed
125   under the star of a galliard.

    ANDREW Ay, 'tis strong, and it does indifferent well in a
127   dun-colored stock. Shall we set about some revels?

    TOBY What shall we do else? Were we not born under
129   Taurus?

130 ANDREW Taurus? That's sides and heart.

    TOBY No, sir; it is legs and thighs. Let me see thee caper.
    Ha, higher; ha, ha, excellent!   *Exeunt.*

                              *

∽ **I.4** *Enter Valentine, and Viola in man's attire.*

    VALENTINE If the duke continue these favors towards
2   you, Cesario, you are like to be much advanced. He
    hath known you but three days and already you are no
    stranger.

5   VIOLA You either fear his humor or my negligence, that
    you call in question the continuance of his love. Is he
    inconstant, sir, in his favors?

    VALENTINE No, believe me.

---

115 *back-trick* backward step in a dance 118 *take* collect 119 *Mistress
Mall's picture* any woman's portrait 120 *coranto* swift running dance 122
sink-a-pace rapid dance of five steps (French *cinque-pas*) 125 *under . . . galliard* i.e., under a dancing star 127 *stock* stocking 129 *Taurus* the Bull,
one of the signs of the zodiac, which governed the nose and throat
    I.4 The palace of Duke Orsino 2 *advanced* promoted 5 *humor* change-
ableness

Enter Duke, Curio, and Attendants.

VIOLA I thank you. Here comes the count.

DUKE Who saw Cesario, ho?   *10*

VIOLA On your attendance, my lord, here.

DUKE *[To Curio and Attendants]*

Stand you awhile aloof. *[To Cesario]* Cesario,   *12*

Thou know'st no less but all. I have unclasped   *13*

To thee the book even of my secret soul.

Therefore, good youth, address thy gait unto her;   *15*

Be not denied access, stand at her doors,

And tell them there thy fixèd foot shall grow

Till thou have audience.

VIOLA   Sure, my noble lord,

If she be so abandoned to her sorrow

As it is spoke, she never will admit me.   *20*

DUKE

Be clamorous and leap all civil bounds

Rather than make unprofited return.

VIOLA

Say I do speak with her, my lord, what then?

DUKE

O, then unfold the passion of my love;

Surprise her with discourse of my dear faith;   *25*

It shall become thee well to act my woes.

She will attend it better in thy youth

Than in a nuncio's of more grave aspect.   *28*

VIOLA

I think not so, my lord.

DUKE   Dear lad, believe it;

For they shall yet belie thy happy years   *30*

That say thou art a man. Diana's lip   *31*

Is not more smooth and rubious; thy small pipe   *32*

---

12 *you* i.e., all except Cesario   13 *no less but all* everything   15 *address thy gait* direct your steps   25 *Surprise* ambush   28 *nuncio's* messenger's   31 *Diana* Roman goddess of hunting and protector of women's chastity   32 *rubious* ruby red; *pipe* throat, voice

33   Is as the maiden's organ, shrill and sound,
34   And all is semblative a woman's part.
35   I know thy constellation is right apt
      For this affair. Some four or five attend him,
      All, if you will; for I myself am best
      When least in company. Prosper well in this,
      And thou shalt live as freely as thy lord
40   To call his fortunes thine.
      VIOLA   I'll do my best
41   To woo your lady. *[Aside]* Yet a barful strife!
      Whoe'er I woo, myself would be his wife.   *Exeunt.*

                              *

∿ **I.5** *Enter Maria and Clown.*

      MARIA   Nay, either tell me where thou hast been, or I will
      not open my lips so wide as a bristle may enter in way
      of thy excuse. My lady will hang thee for thy absence.
4   CLOWN   Let her hang me. He that is well hanged in this
5   world needs to fear no colors.
6   MARIA   Make that good.
      CLOWN   He shall see none to fear.
8   MARIA   A good lenten answer. I can tell thee where that
      saying was born, of "I fear no colors."
10   CLOWN   Where, good Mistress Mary?
      MARIA   In the wars; and that may you be bold to say in
      your foolery.
      CLOWN   Well, God give them wisdom that have it, and
      those that are fools, let them use their talents.
      MARIA   Yet you will be hanged for being so long absent.
      Or to be turned away: is not that as good as a hanging
      to you?

---

33 *shrill and sound* high and clear   34 *semblative* like   35 *constellation* pre-
destined nature   41 *barful strife* conflict full of hindrances
      I.5 Within the house of Olivia   4 *well hanged* (the hanged man prover-
bially has nothing more to fear, but here also "well hung")   5 *fear no colors*
fear nothing (proverbial)   6 *Make that good* "explain," but also "clean up
your language"   8 *lenten* scanty, chastened

CLOWN   Many a good hanging prevents a bad marriage,
and for turning away, let summer bear it out.   19

MARIA   You are resolute then?   20

CLOWN   Not so, neither; but I am resolved on two
points.   22

MARIA   That if one break, the other will hold; or if both   23
break, your gaskins fall.   24

CLOWN   Apt, in good faith; very apt. Well, go thy way! If
Sir Toby would leave drinking, thou wert as witty a
piece of Eve's flesh as any in Illyria.   27

MARIA   Peace, you rogue; no more o' that. Here comes
my lady. Make your excuse wisely, you were best. *[Exit.]*   29
Enter Lady Olivia with Malvolio.

CLOWN   Wit, an't be thy will, put me into good fooling.   30
Those wits that think they have thee do very oft prove
fools, and I that am sure I lack thee may pass for a wise
man. For what says Quinapalus? "Better a witty fool   33
than a foolish wit." God bless thee, lady.

OLIVIA   Take the fool away.

CLOWN   Do you not hear, fellows? Take away the lady.

OLIVIA   Go to, you're a dry fool! I'll no more of you. Be-   37
sides, you grow dishonest.   38

CLOWN   Two faults, madonna, that drink and good   39
counsel will amend. For give the dry fool drink, then is   40
the fool not dry. Bid the dishonest man mend himself: 41
if he mend, he is no longer dishonest; if he cannot, let
the botcher mend him. Anything that's mended is but   43
patched; virtue that transgresses is but patched with
sin, and sin that amends is but patched with virtue. If
that this simple syllogism will serve, so; if it will not,   46

---

19 *let . . . out* i.e., let mild weather make homelessness endurable   22 *points*
laces fastening hose to doublet   23–24 *if one . . . fall* (Maria puns on
"points," l. 22)   24 *gaskins* loose breeches   27 *Eve's flesh* erring woman   29
you were best it would be best for you   33 *Quinapalus* (an invention of the
clown)   37 *Go to* enough, cease; *dry* dull   38 *dishonest* unreliable   39
madonna my lady (ironic)   41 *dry* thirsty   43 *botcher* mender of clothes
46 *syllogism* three-step logical argument in set form

47   what remedy? As there is no true cuckold but calamity,
      so beauty's a flower. The lady bade take away the fool;
      therefore, I say again, take her away.

50 OLIVIA   Sir, I bade them take away you.

51 CLOWN   Misprision in the highest degree. Lady, *cucullus
      non facit monachum*. That's as much to say as, I wear
53   not motley in my brain. Good madonna, give me leave
      to prove you a fool.

    OLIVIA   Can you do it?

56 CLOWN   Dexteriously, good madonna.

    OLIVIA   Make your proof.

58 CLOWN   I must catechize you for it, madonna. Good my
59   mouse of virtue, answer me.

60 OLIVIA   Well, sir, for want of other idleness, I'll bide your
      proof.

    CLOWN   Good madonna, why mourn'st thou?

    OLIVIA   Good fool, for my brother's death.

    CLOWN   I think his soul is in hell, madonna.

    OLIVIA   I know his soul is in heaven, fool.

    CLOWN   The more fool, madonna, to mourn for your
      brother's soul, being in heaven. Take away the fool,
      gentlemen.

    OLIVIA   What think you of this fool, Malvolio? Doth he
70   not mend?

    MALVOLIO   Yes, and shall do till the pangs of death shake
      him. Infirmity, that decays the wise, doth ever make the
      better fool.

    CLOWN   God send you, sir, a speedy infirmity, for the
      better increasing your folly. Sir Toby will be sworn that
      I am no fox, but he will not pass his word for twopence
      that you are no fool.

47–48 *As . . . flower* (obscure, but apparently proverbial reassurance that the
young and beautiful Olivia will not remain solitary)   51 *Misprision* error
51–52 *cucullus . . . monachum* the cowl doesn't make the monk   53 *motley*
clothing of a mixed color, worn by stage fools   56 *Dexteriously* (variant of
"dexterously")   58 *catechize* question   59 *mouse* (term of endearment); *of
virtue* virtuous

OLIVIA   How say you to that, Malvolio?

MALVOLIO   I marvel your ladyship takes delight in such a
barren rascal. I saw him put down the other day with   *80*
an ordinary fool that has no more brain than a stone.
Look you now, he's out of his guard already. Unless you   *82*
laugh and minister occasion to him, he is gagged. I   *83*
protest I take these wise men that crow so at these set   *84*
kind of fools no better than the fools' zanies.   *85*

OLIVIA   O, you are sick of self-love, Malvolio, and taste
with a distempered appetite. To be generous, guiltless,
and of free disposition, is to take those things for bird-   *88*
bolts that you deem cannon bullets. There is no slander
in an allowed fool, though he do nothing but rail; nor   *90*
no railing in a known discreet man, though he do
nothing but reprove.

CLOWN   Now Mercury indue thee with leasing, for thou   *93*
speak'st well of fools.

   Enter Maria.

MARIA   Madam, there is at the gate a young gentleman
much desires to speak with you.

OLIVIA   From the count Orsino, is it?

MARIA   I know not, madam. 'Tis a fair young man, and
well attended.

OLIVIA   Who of my people hold him in delay?   *100*

MARIA   Sir Toby, madam, your kinsman.

OLIVIA   Fetch him off, I pray you. He speaks nothing but
madman. Fie on him! *[Exit Maria.]* Go you, Malvolio.
If it be a suit from the count, I am sick, or not at
home. What you will, to dismiss it.   *Exit Malvolio.*
Now you see, sir, how your fooling grows old, and   *106*
people dislike it.

---

82 *out of his guard* without a defense (of wit)   83 *minister occasion* give an
opportunity   84 *set* with a rehearsed patter   85 *zanies* i.e., fools' assistants
88–89 *bird-bolts* blunt-headed arrows for shooting birds   90 *allowed* licensed   93 *Mercury* god of guile and tricks; *indue . . . leasing* endow you
with the art of casuistry   106 *old* stale

CLOWN   Thou hast spoke for us, madonna, as if thy el-
dest son should be a fool; whose skull Jove cram with
110   brains, for – here he comes – one of thy kin has a most
111   weak pia mater.
　　Enter Sir Toby.
OLIVIA   By mine honor, half drunk. What is he at the
gate, cousin?
TOBY   A gentleman.
OLIVIA   A gentleman? What gentleman?
TOBY   'Tis a gentleman here. A plague o' these pickle-
herring! How now, sot?
CLOWN   Good Sir Toby.
OLIVIA   Cousin, cousin, how have you come so early by
120   this lethargy?
TOBY   Lechery? I defy lechery. There's one at the gate.
OLIVIA   Ay, marry, what is he?
TOBY   Let him be the devil an he will, I care not. Give
124   me faith, say I. Well, it's all one.　　　　　　*Exit.*
OLIVIA   What's a drunken man like, fool?
CLOWN   Like a drowned man, a fool, and a madman.
127   One draft above heat makes him a fool, the second
mads him, and a third drowns him.
129 OLIVIA   Go thou and seek the crowner, and let him sit o'
130   my coz; for he's in the third degree of drink – he's
drowned. Go look after him.
CLOWN   He is but mad yet, madonna, and the fool shall
look to the madman.　　　　　　　　　　*[Exit.]*
　　Enter Malvolio.
MALVOLIO   Madam, yond young fellow swears he will
speak with you. I told him you were sick; he takes on
him to understand so much, and therefore comes to
speak with you. I told him you were asleep; he seems to

---

111 *pia mater* i.e., brain　120 *lethargy* sickness　124 *faith* i.e., to resist the
devil　127 *above heat* above the amount to make him normally warm　129
crowner coroner　129–30 *sit o' my coz* hold an inquest on my kinsman (Sir
Toby)

have a foreknowledge of that too, and therefore comes
to speak with you. What is to be said to him, lady? He's
fortified against any denial.   140

OLIVIA   Tell him he shall not speak with me.

MALVOLIO   Has been told so; and he says he'll stand at   142
your door like a sheriff's post, and be the supporter to a   143
bench, but he'll speak with you.

OLIVIA   What kind o' man is he?

MALVOLIO   Why, of mankind.

OLIVIA   What manner of man?

MALVOLIO   Of very ill manner. He'll speak with you, will
you or no.

OLIVIA   Of what personage and years is he?   150

MALVOLIO   Not yet old enough for a man nor young
enough for a boy; as a squash is before 'tis a peasecod,   152
or a codling when 'tis almost an apple. 'Tis with him in   153
standing water, between boy and man. He is very well-   154
favored and he speaks very shrewishly. One would
think his mother's milk were scarce out of him.

OLIVIA   Let him approach. Call in my gentlewoman.

MALVOLIO   Gentlewoman, my lady calls.   *Exit.*
     Enter Maria.

OLIVIA   Give me my veil; come, throw it o'er my face.
We'll once more hear Orsino's embassy.   160
     Enter Viola.

VIOLA   The honorable lady of the house, which is she?

OLIVIA   Speak to me; I shall answer for her. Your will?

VIOLA   Most radiant, exquisite, and unmatchable
beauty – I pray you tell me if this be the lady of the
house, for I never saw her – I would be loath to cast
away my speech; for, besides that it is excellently well
penned, I have taken great pains to con it. Good beau-   167

---

142 *Has* he has (from "h' has")   143 *sheriff's post* post before a sheriff's house
on which notices were posted   152 *squash* unripe pea pod; *peasecod* ripe pea
pod   153 *codling* unripe apple   154 *standing water* the tide at ebb or flood
when it flows neither way   167 *con* memorize

)

168   ties, let me sustain no scorn. I am very comptible, even
to the least sinister usage.

170 OLIVIA   Whence came you, sir?

VIOLA   I can say little more than I have studied, and that
question's out of my part. Good gentle one, give me
modest assurance if you be the lady of the house, that I
may proceed in my speech.

175 OLIVIA   Are you a comedian?

VIOLA   No, my profound heart; and yet (by the very
fangs of malice I swear) I am not that I play. Are you
the lady of the house?

179 OLIVIA   If I do not usurp myself, I am.

180 VIOLA   Most certain, if you are she, you do usurp yourself; for what is yours to bestow is not yours to reserve.

182   But this is from my commission. I will on with my
speech in your praise and then show you the heart of
my message.

185 OLIVIA   Come to what is important in't. I forgive you the
praise.

VIOLA   Alas, I took great pains to study it; and 'tis
poetical.

OLIVIA   It is the more like to be feigned; I pray you keep
190   it in. I heard you were saucy at my gates; and allowed
your approach rather to wonder at you than to hear
192   you. If you be not mad, be gone; if you have reason, be
193   brief. 'Tis not that time of moon with me to make one
194   in so skipping a dialogue.

MARIA   Will you hoist sail, sir? Here lies your way.

196 VIOLA   No, good swabber; I am to hull here a little
197   longer. Some mollification for your giant, sweet lady.
Tell me your mind. I am a messenger.

OLIVIA   Sure you have some hideous matter to deliver,
200   when the courtesy of it is so fearful. Speak your office.

---

168 *sustain* endure; *comptible* sensitive   175 *comedian* actor   179 *usurp* sup-
plant   182 *from* outside   185 *forgive* excuse   192 *reason* sanity   193
'Tis . . . me i.e., I am not in the mood   194 *skipping* sprightly   196 *swabber*
one who washes decks; *hull* float without sail   197 *giant* i.e., the small Maria
200 *courtesy* formality; *office* business

VIOLA   It alone concerns your ear. I bring no overture of   *201*
war, no taxation of homage. I hold the olive in my   *202*
hand. My words are as full of peace as matter.

OLIVIA   Yet you began rudely. What are you? What
would you?

VIOLA   The rudeness that hath appeared in me have I
learned from my entertainment. What I am, and what   *207*
I would, are as secret as maidenhead: to your ears, di-   *208*
vinity; to any other's, profanation.

OLIVIA   Give us the place alone; we will hear this divin-   *210*
ity. *[Exit Maria.]* Now, sir, what is your text?

VIOLA   Most sweet lady –

OLIVIA   A comfortable doctrine, and much may be said   *213*
of it. Where lies your text?

VIOLA   In Orsino's bosom.

OLIVIA   In his bosom? In what chapter of his bosom?

VIOLA   To answer by the method, in the first of his heart.   *217*

OLIVIA   O, I have read it; it is heresy. Have you no more
to say?

VIOLA   Good madam, let me see your face.   *220*

OLIVIA   Have you any commission from your lord to ne-
gotiate with my face? You are now out of your text. But
we will draw the curtain and show you the picture.
[Unveils.] Look you, sir, such a one I was this present.   *224*
Is't not well done?

VIOLA   Excellently done, if God did all.

OLIVIA   'Tis in grain, sir; 'twill endure wind and weather.   *227*

VIOLA
'Tis beauty truly blent, whose red and white
Nature's own sweet and cunning hand laid on.   *229*
Lady, you are the cruel'st she alive   *230*
If you will lead these graces to the grave,
And leave the world no copy.

---

201 *overture* declaration   202 *taxation* demand   207 *entertainment* reception   208–9 *divinity* a holy message   213 *comfortable* comforting   217
To . . . method to continue the figure   224 *this present* a minute ago   227 *in
grain* fast dyed   229 *cunning* skillful

OLIVIA   O, sir, I will not be so hard-hearted. I will give
234   out divers schedules of my beauty. It shall be invento-
235   ried, and every particle and utensil labeled to my will:
236   as, item, two lips, indifferent red; item, two gray eyes,
       with lids to them; item, one neck, one chin, and so
       forth. Were you sent hither to praise me?

VIOLA
       I see you what you are; you are too proud;
240   But if you were the devil, you are fair.
       My lord and master loves you. O, such love
242   Could be but recompensed though you were crowned
243   The nonpareil of beauty.

OLIVIA   How does he love me?

VIOLA
244   With adorations, fertile tears,
       With groans that thunder love, with sighs of fire.

OLIVIA
       Your lord does know my mind; I cannot love him.
       Yet I suppose him virtuous, know him noble,
       Of great estate, of fresh and stainless youth;
249   In voices well divulged, free, learned, and valiant,
250   And in dimension and the shape of nature
       A gracious person. But yet I cannot love him.
       He might have took his answer long ago.

VIOLA
       If I did love you in my master's flame,
254   With such a suff'ring, such a deadly life,
       In your denial I would find no sense;
       I would not understand it.

OLIVIA   Why, what would you?

VIOLA
257   Make me a willow cabin at your gate.

---

234 *schedules* lists   235 *utensil* article; *labeled to* added to   236 *item* namely;
indifferent moderately   240 *if* even if   242 *but recompensed though* no more
than repaid even though   243 *nonpareil* unequaled one   244 *fertile* abun-
dant   249 *In voices well divulged* in public opinion well reported   254
deadly life life that is like death   257 *willow* (symbol of grief for unrequited
love)

And call upon my soul within the house;
Write loyal cantons of contemnèd love   259
And sing them loud even in the dead of night;   260
Hallo your name to the reverberate hills
And make the babbling gossip of the air   262
Cry out "Olivia!" O, you should not rest
Between the elements of air and earth
But you should pity me.

OLIVIA
You might do much. What is your parentage?

VIOLA
Above my fortunes, yet my state is well.
I am a gentleman.

OLIVIA   Get you to your lord.
I cannot love him. Let him send no more,
Unless, perchance, you come to me again   270
To tell me how he takes it. Fare you well.
I thank you for your pains. Spend this for me.

VIOLA
I am no fee'd post, lady; keep your purse;   273
My master, not myself, lacks recompense.
Love make his heart of flint that you shall love;
And let your fervor, like my master's, be
Placed in contempt. Farewell, fair cruelty.   *Exit.*

OLIVIA
"What is your parentage?"
"Above my fortunes, yet my state is well.
I am a gentleman." I'll be sworn thou art.   280
Thy tongue, thy face, thy limbs, actions, and spirit
Do give thee fivefold blazon. Not too fast; soft, soft,   282
Unless the master were the man. How now?   283
Even so quickly may one catch the plague?
Methinks I feel this youth's perfections
With an invisible and subtle stealth

---

259 *cantons* songs; *contemnèd* rejected   262 *babbling gossip* echo   273 *fee'd
post* messenger to be paid or tipped   282 *blazon* heraldic identification, as
on a shield   283 *Unless . . . man* i.e., unless Orsino were Cesario

To creep in at mine eyes. Well, let it be.
What ho, Malvolio!
   Enter Malvolio.

MALVOLIO   Here, madam, at your service.

OLIVIA
  Run after that same peevish messenger,
290 The county's man. He left this ring behind him,
  Would I or not. Tell him I'll none of it.
292 Desire him not to flatter with his lord
  Nor hold him up with hopes. I am not for him.
  If that the youth will come this way tomorrow,
  I'll give him reasons for't. Hie thee, Malvolio.

MALVOLIO
  Madam, I will.   *Exit.*

OLIVIA
  I do I know not what, and fear to find
  Mine eye too great a flatterer for my mind.
299 Fate, show thy force; ourselves we do not owe.
300 What is decreed must be – and be this so!   *[Exit.]*
                         *

∾ **II.1** *Enter Antonio and Sebastian.*

ANTONIO   Will you stay no longer? Nor will you not that
    I go with you?
3 SEBASTIAN   By your patience, no. My stars shine darkly
4   over me; the malignancy of my fate might perhaps dis-
    temper yours. Therefore I shall crave of you your leave,
    that I may bear my evils alone. It were a bad recom-
    pense for your love to lay any of them on you.

ANTONIO   Let me yet know of you whither you are
    bound.

---

290 *county* count   292 *flatter with* encourage   299 *owe* own
   II.1 A lodging some distance from Orsino's court   3 *patience* leave   4–5
distemper disturb

SEBASTIAN   No, sooth, sir. My determinate voyage is   10
   mere extravagancy. But I perceive in you so excellent a   11
   touch of modesty that you will not extort from me
   what I am willing to keep in; therefore it charges me in   13
   manners the rather to express myself. You must know
   of me then, Antonio, my name is Sebastian, which I
   called Roderigo. My father was that Sebastian of Mes-   16
   saline whom I know you have heard of. He left behind
   him myself and a sister, both born in an hour. If the   18
   heavens had been pleased, would we had so ended! But
   you, sir, altered that, for some hour before you took me   20
   from the breach of the sea was my sister drowned.   21

ANTONIO   Alas the day!

SEBASTIAN   A lady, sir, though it was said she much re-
   sembled me, was yet of many accounted beautiful. But
   though I could not with such estimable wonder overfar   25
   believe that, yet thus far I will boldly publish her: she   26
   bore a mind that envy could not but call fair. She is
   drowned already, sir, with salt water, though I seem to
   drown her remembrance again with more.

ANTONIO   Pardon me, sir, your bad entertainment.   30

SEBASTIAN   O good Antonio, forgive me your trouble.   31

ANTONIO   If you will not murder me for my love, let me   32
   be your servant.

SEBASTIAN   If you will not undo what you have done,
   that is, kill him whom you have recovered, desire it not.   35
   Fare ye well at once. My bosom is full of kindness, and
   I am yet so near the manners of my mother that, upon   37
   the least occasion more, mine eyes will tell tales of me.
   I am bound to the Count Orsino's court. Farewell.
                                       Exit.

10 *sooth* truly; *determinate* determined upon   **11** *extravagancy* wandering
13–14 *it . . . manners* I am compelled in good manners   **16–17** *Messaline*
Messina in Sicily   **18** *in an hour* in the same hour   **21** *the breach of the sea*
the breaking waves   **25** *estimable wonder* admiring judgment   **26** *publish*
describe publicly   **30** *entertainment* treatment as my guest   **31** *your trouble*
for causing you trouble   **32** *murder me for* be my death in return for   **35** *recovered* saved   **37–38** *so near . . . tales of me* so effeminate I shall weep

ANTONIO
40   The gentleness of all the gods go with thee.
    I have many enemies in Orsino's court,
    Else would I very shortly see thee there.
    But come what may, I do adore thee so
    That danger shall seem sport, and I will go.   *Exit.*

*

∾ **II.2** *Enter Viola and Malvolio at several doors.*

MALVOLIO Were not you ev'n now with the Countess
Olivia?
VIOLA Even now, sir. On a moderate pace I have since
arrived but hither.
MALVOLIO She returns this ring to you, sir. You might
have saved me my pains, to have taken it away yourself.
She adds, moreover, that you should put your lord into
8   a desperate assurance she will none of him. And one
thing more, that you be never so hardy to come again
10   in his affairs, unless it be to report your lord's taking of
this. Receive it so.
VIOLA She took the ring of me. I'll none of it.
MALVOLIO Come, sir, you peevishly threw it to her, and
her will is, it should be so returned. If it be worth
stooping for, there it lies, in your eye; if not, be it his
that finds it.   *Exit.*
VIOLA
    I left no ring with her. What means this lady?
    Fortune forbid my outside have not charmed her.
19   She made good view of me; indeed, so much
20   That, as methought, her eyes had lost her tongue,
21   For she did speak in starts distractedly.
22   She loves me sure; the cunning of her passion
    Invites me in this churlish messenger.

II.2 A street near Olivia's house **s.d.** *several* different **8** *desperate* without
hope **19** *made good view of* looked intently at **20** *lost* caused her to lose
21 *distractedly* madly **22** *cunning* craftiness

None of my lord's ring? Why, he sent her none.
I am the man. If it be so, as 'tis,
Poor lady, she were better love a dream.   26
Disguise, I see thou art a wickedness
Wherein the pregnant enemy does much.   28
How easy is it for the proper false   29
In women's waxen hearts to set their forms!   30
Alas, our frailty is the cause, not we,
For such as we are made of, such we be.
How will this fadge? My master loves her dearly;   33
And I (poor monster) fond as much on him;   34
And she (mistaken) seems to dote on me.
What will become of this? As I am man,
My state is desperate for my master's love.   37
As I am woman (now alas the day!),
What thriftless sighs shall poor Olivia breathe?   39
O Time, thou must untangle this, not I;   40
It is too hard a knot for me t' untie.   *[Exit.]*
                        *

∾ **II.3** *Enter Sir Toby and Sir Andrew.*

TOBY   Approach, Sir Andrew. Not to be abed after mid-
    night is to be up betimes; and *"diluculo surgere,"* thou   2
    know'st.
ANDREW   Nay, by my troth, I know not, but I know to
    be up late is to be up late.
TOBY   A false conclusion; I hate it as an unfilled can. To   6
    be up after midnight, and to go to bed then, is early; so
    that to go to bed after midnight is to go to bed betimes.
    Does not our lives consist of the four elements?

---

26 *were better* would do better to   28 *pregnant enemy* resourceful Satan   29
the proper false deceivers who are prepossessing in appearance   30 *forms* impressions (as of a seal)   33 *fadge* turn out   34 *monster* (because both man
and woman); *fond* dote   37 *desperate* hopeless   39 *thriftless* unprofitable
    II.3 Within Olivia's house   2 *diluculo surgere [saluberrimum est]* to get up
at dawn is healthful (Lily's *Latin Grammar*)   6 *can* metal vessel for holding
liquor

10 ANDREW   Faith, so they say; but I think it rather consists
       of eating and drinking.

    TOBY   Thou'rt a scholar! Let us therefore eat and drink.
13   Marian I say! a stoup of wine!
       Enter Clown.

    ANDREW   Here comes the fool, i' faith.

15 CLOWN   How now, my hearts? Did you never see the pic-
       ture of We Three?

17 TOBY   Welcome, ass. Now let's have a catch.

18 ANDREW   By my troth, the fool has an excellent breast. I
       had rather than forty shillings I had such a leg, and so
20   sweet a breath to sing, as the fool has. In sooth, thou
21   wast in very gracious fooling last night, when thou
22   spok'st of Pigrogromitus, of the Vapians passing the
       equinoctial of Queubus. 'Twas very good, i' faith. I sent
24   thee sixpence for thy leman. Hadst it?

25 CLOWN   I did impeticos thy gratillity, for Malvolio's nose
       is no whipstock. My lady has a white hand, and the
27   Myrmidons are no bottle-ale houses.

    ANDREW   Excellent. Why, this is the best fooling, when
       all is done. Now a song!

30 TOBY   Come on! there is sixpence for you. Let's have a
       song.

32 ANDREW   There's a testril of me too. If one knight give a –

33 CLOWN   Would you have a love song, or a song of good
       life?

    TOBY   A love song, a love song.

    ANDREW   Ay, ay, I care not for good life.

---

13 *stoup* large drinking vessel   15 *hearts* (term of endearment)   15–16
picture of We Three picture showing two fools or asses inscribed "We
Three," the onlooker making the third   17 *catch* round song (such as
"Three Blind Mice")   18 *breast* voice   21 *gracious* elegant   22–23 *Pigrogromitus . . . Queubus* (meaningless mock-learning)   24 *leman* sweetheart
25 *impeticos* put in pocket of gown; *gratillity* gratuity   25–26 *for . . . whip-
stock* i.e., Malvolio sticks his nose into everything (?)   27 *Myrmidons* Thes-
salian warriors; i.e., not mermaids on tavern signs (?)   32 *testril* tester,
sixpence   33–34 *good life* virtuous living

Clown sings.
　O mistress mine, where are you roaming?
　O, stay and hear! your true-love's coming,
　　That can sing both high and low.
　Trip no further, pretty sweeting;　　　　　　　　　*40*
　Journeys end in lovers' meeting,
　　Every wise man's son doth know.

ANDREW　Excellent good, i' faith.

TOBY　Good, good.

Clown [sings].
　What is love? 'Tis not hereafter;
　Present mirth hath present laughter;
　　What's to come is still unsure:
　In delay there lies no plenty;
　Then come kiss me, sweet and twenty,
　　Youth's a stuff will not endure.　　　　　　　　*50*

ANDREW　A mellifluous voice, as I am true knight.

TOBY　A contagious breath.

ANDREW　Very sweet and contagious, i' faith.

TOBY　To hear by the nose, it is dulcet in contagion. But　*54*
　shall we make the welkin dance indeed? Shall we rouse　*55*
　the night owl in a catch that will draw three souls out
　of one weaver? Shall we do that?　　　　　　　　*57*

ANDREW　An you love me, let's do't. I am dog at a catch.　*58*

CLOWN　By'r Lady, sir, and some dogs will catch well.

ANDREW　Most certain. Let our catch be "Thou knave."　*60*

CLOWN　"Hold thy peace, thou knave," knight? I shall be
　constrained in't to call thee knave, knight.

ANDREW　'Tis not the first time I have constrained one to
　call me knave. Begin, fool. It begins, "Hold thy peace."

CLOWN　I shall never begin if I hold my peace.

ANDREW　Good, i' faith! Come, begin.

　Catch sung. Enter Maria.

---

54 *dulcet* sweet　**55** *welkin* sky　**57** *weaver* (weavers were famous for psalm
singing)　**58** *dog* good at

MARIA What a caterwauling do you keep here? If my
lady have not called up her steward Malvolio and bid
him turn you out of doors, never trust me.

70 TOBY My lady's a Cataian, we are politicians, Malvolio's
71 a Peg-a-Ramsey, and *[Sings.]* "Three merry men be
72 we." Am not I consanguineous? Am I not of her blood?
73 Tilly-vally, lady. *[Sings.]* "There dwelt a man in Baby-
lon, lady, lady."

CLOWN Beshrew me, the knight's in admirable fooling.

ANDREW Ay, he does well enough if he be disposed, and
so do I too. He does it with a better grace, but I do it
78 more natural.

TOBY *[Sings.]*
"O the twelfth day of December."

80 MARIA For the love o' God, peace!
   Enter Malvolio.

MALVOLIO My masters, are you mad? Or what are you?
Have you no wit, manners, nor honesty, but to gabble
like tinkers at this time of night? Do ye make an alehouse
84 of my lady's house, that ye squeak out your coziers'
85 catches without any mitigation or remorse of voice? Is
there no respect of place, persons, nor time in you?

87 TOBY We did keep time, sir, in our catches. Sneck up.

88 MALVOLIO Sir Toby, I must be round with you. My lady
bade me tell you that, though she harbors you as her
90 kinsman, she's nothing allied to your disorders. If you
can separate yourself and your misdemeanors, you are
welcome to the house. If not, and it would please you to
take leave of her, she is very willing to bid you farewell.

TOBY *[Sings.]*
94 "Farewell, dear heart, since I must needs be gone."

---

70 *Cataian* native of Cathay, trickster; *politicians* intriguers 71 *Peg-a-Ram-sey* disreputable woman in an old song 72 *consanguineous* related 73 *Tilly-vally* nonsense; *There dwelt* ... (from an old song, "The Constancy of Susanna") 78 *natural* naturally (but the word also means "like a fool") 84 *coziers'* cobblers' 85 *mitigation or remorse* i.e., considerate lowering 87 *Sneck up* go hang 88 *round* plain 94 *Farewell, dear heart* ... (from an old song, "Corydon's Farewell to Phyllis")

MARIA   Nay, good Sir Toby.
CLOWN   *[Sings.]*
   "His eyes do show his days are almost done."
MALVOLIO   Is't even so?
TOBY   *[Sings.]*
   "But I will never die."
CLOWN   *[Sings.]*
   Sir Toby, there you lie.
MALVOLIO   This is much credit to you.   *100*
TOBY   *[Sings.]*
   "Shall I bid him go?"
CLOWN   *[Sings.]*
   "What an if you do?"
TOBY   *[Sings.]*
   "Shall I bid him go, and spare not?"
CLOWN   *[Sings.]*
   "O, no, no, no, no, you dare not!"
TOBY   Out o' tune, sir? Ye lie. Art any more than a stew-
   ard? Dost thou think, because thou art virtuous, there
   shall be no more cakes and ale?
CLOWN   Yes, by Saint Anne, and ginger shall be hot i' th'   108
   mouth too.
TOBY   Thou'rt i' th' right. – Go, sir, rub your chain with   110
   crumbs. A stoup of wine, Maria!   111
MALVOLIO   Mistress Mary, if you prized my lady's favor
   at anything more than contempt, you would not give   113
   means for this uncivil rule. She shall know of it, by this
   hand.   *Exit.*
MARIA   Go shake your ears.   116
ANDREW   'Twere as good a deed as to drink when a man's
   ahungry, to challenge him the field, and then to break
   promise with him and make a fool of him.

---

108 *Saint Anne* mother of the Virgin Mary; *ginger* (used to spice ale)
110–11 *rub . . . crumbs* (a contemptuous allusion to his steward's chain)
111 *stoup* large drinking vessel   **113–14** *give means* i.e., bring the wine   **116**
your ears i.e., your ass's ears

120 TOBY   Do't, knight. I'll write thee a challenge; or I'll deliver thy indignation to him by word of mouth.

MARIA   Sweet Sir Toby, be patient for tonight. Since the
youth of the count's was today with my lady, she is
much out of quiet. For Monsieur Malvolio, let me
125 alone with him. If I do not gull him into a nayword,
126 and make him a common recreation, do not think I
have wit enough to lie straight in my bed. I know I can
do it.

129 TOBY   Possess us, possess us. Tell us something of him.

130 MARIA   Marry, sir, sometimes he is a kind of Puritan.

ANDREW   O, if I thought that, I'd beat him like a dog.

TOBY   What, for being a Puritan? Thy exquisite reason,
dear knight.

ANDREW   I have no exquisite reason for't, but I have reason good enough.

MARIA   The devil a Puritan that he is, or anything con-
137 stantly but a time-pleaser; an affectioned ass, that cons
138 state without book and utters it by great swarths; the
best persuaded of himself; so crammed, as he thinks,
140 with excellencies that it is his grounds of faith that all
that look on him love him; and on that vice in him will
my revenge find notable cause to work.

TOBY   What wilt thou do?

MARIA   I will drop in his way some obscure epistles of
love, wherein by the color of his beard, the shape of his
146 leg, the manner of his gait, the expressure of his eye,
forehead, and complexion, he shall find himself most
148 feelingly personated. I can write very like my lady your
niece; on a forgotten matter we can hardly make dis-
150 tinction of our hands.

151 TOBY   Excellent. I smell a device.

---

125 *gull* trick; *nayword* byword   126 *recreation* amusement   129 *Possess us*
give us the facts   130 *Puritan* member of a strict Protestant faction generally
opposed to playgoing, reveling, etc.   137 *time-pleaser* sycophant; *affectioned*
affected   137–38 *cons . . . book* learns statecraft   138 *swarths* quantities
146 *expressure* expression   148 *personated* represented   151 *device* trick,
stratagem

ANDREW   I have't in my nose too.

TOBY   He shall think by the letters that thou wilt drop that they come from my niece, and that she's in love with him.

MARIA   My purpose is indeed a horse of that color.

ANDREW   And your horse now would make him an ass.

MARIA   Ass, I doubt not.

ANDREW   O, 'twill be admirable.

MARIA   Sport royal, I warrant you. I know my physic will   *160*
work with him. I will plant you two, and let the fool make a third, where he shall find the letter. Observe his construction of it. For this night, to bed, and dream on   163
the event. Farewell.   *Exit.*   164

TOBY   Good night, Penthesilea.   165

ANDREW   Before me, she's a good wench.   166

TOBY   She's a beagle true-bred, and one that adores me.   167
What o' that?

ANDREW   I was adored once too.

TOBY   Let's to bed, knight. Thou hadst need send for   *170*
more money.

ANDREW   If I cannot recover your niece, I am a foul way   172
out.   173

TOBY   Send for money, knight. If thou hast her not i' th'
end, call me Cut.   175

ANDREW   If I do not, never trust me, take it how you will.

TOBY   Come, come; I'll go burn some sack. 'Tis too late   178
to go to bed now. Come, knight; come, knight.
                                                Exeunt.

*

---

163 *construction* interpretation   164 *event* outcome   165 *Penthesilea* queen of the Amazons   166 *Before me* I swear by myself   167 *beagle* small rabbit hound   172 *recover* gain   173 *out* out of money   175 *Cut* horse with a docked tail; also, a gelding   178 *burn some sack* warm some sherry

◡ II.4 *Enter Duke, Viola, Curio, and others.*

DUKE
    Give me some music. Now good morrow, friends.
    Now, good Cesario, but that piece of song,
3   That old and antic song we heard last night.
    Methought it did relieve my passion much,
5   More than light airs and recollected terms
    Of these most brisk and giddy-pacèd times.
    Come, but one verse.
    CURIO He is not here, so please your lordship, that
    should sing it.
10 DUKE Who was it?
    CURIO Feste the jester, my lord, a fool that the Lady
    Olivia's father took much delight in. He is about the
    house.
DUKE
    Seek him out, and play the tune the while.
                                  [Exit Curio.]
    Music plays.
    Come hither, boy. If ever thou shalt love,
    In the sweet pangs of it remember me;
    For such as I am all true lovers are,
18   Unstaid and skittish in all motions else
    Save in the constant image of the creature
20   That is beloved. How dost thou like this tune?
VIOLA
21   It gives a very echo to the seat
    Where Love is throned.
    DUKE   Thou dost speak masterly.
    My life upon't, young though thou art, thine eye
24   Hath stayed upon some favor that it loves.
    Hath it not, boy?
    VIOLA   A little, by your favor.

II.4 Within the palace of Orsino **3** *antic* quaint **5** *recollected* studied **18**
motions emotions **21–22** *the seat . . . throned* i.e., the heart **24** *favor* face

DUKE

   What kind of woman is't?

VIOLA   Of your complexion.

DUKE

   She is not worth thee then. What years, i' faith?

VIOLA

   About your years, my lord.

DUKE

   Too old, by heaven! Let still the woman take
   An elder than herself: so wears she to him,   30
   So sways she level in her husband's heart;   31
   For, boy, however we do praise ourselves,
   Our fancies are more giddy and unfirm,   33
   More longing, wavering, sooner lost and worn,
   Than women's are.

VIOLA   I think it well, my lord.

DUKE

   Then let thy love be younger than thyself,
   Or thy affection cannot hold the bent;   37
   For women are as roses, whose fair flow'r,
   Being once displayed, doth fall that very hour.

VIOLA

   And so they are; alas, that they are so.   40
   To die, even when they to perfection grow.
       Enter Curio and Clown.

DUKE

   O, fellow, come, the song we had last night.
   Mark it, Cesario; it is old and plain.
   The spinsters and the knitters in the sun,   44
   And the free maids that weave their thread with bones,   45
   Do use to chant it. It is silly sooth,   46
   And dallies with the innocence of love,
   Like the old age.   48

---

30 *wears* adapts herself   **31** *sways . . . heart* she keeps constant her husband's
love   **33** *fancies* loves   **37** *bent* direction   **44** *spinsters* spinners   **45** *free* in-
nocent; *bones* bone bobbins   **46** *Do use* are accustomed; *silly sooth* simple
truth   **48** *old age* good old days

CLOWN   Are you ready, sir?
50 DUKE   I prithee sing.
         Music.

                    The Song.
         Come away, come away, death,
52   And in sad cypress let me be laid.
         Fly away, fly away, breath;
             I am slain by a fair cruel maid.
55   My shroud of white, stuck all with yew,
             O, prepare it.
57   My part of death, no one so true
             Did share it.

         Not a flower, not a flower sweet,
60   On my black coffin let there be strown;
         Not a friend, not a friend greet
             My poor corpse, where my bones shall be thrown.
         A thousand thousand sighs to save,
             Lay me, O, where
         Sad true lover never find my grave,
             To weep there.

DUKE   There's for thy pains. *[Giving him money]*
CLOWN   No pains, sir. I take pleasure in singing, sir.
DUKE   I'll pay thy pleasure then.
70 CLOWN   Truly, sir, and pleasure will be paid one time or
         another.
DUKE   Give me now leave to leave thee.
73 CLOWN   Now the melancholy god protect thee, and the
74   tailor make thy doublet of changeable taffeta, for thy
         mind is a very opal. I would have men of such con-
         stancy put to sea, that their business might be every-
         thing, and their intent everywhere; for that's it that
78   always makes a good voyage of nothing. Farewell. *Exit.*

———————

52 *cypress* coffin of cypress wood   55 *yew* yew sprigs, associated with mourn-
ing   57 *part* portion   70 *pleasure . . . paid* indulgence exacts its penalty   73
melancholy god (usually identified by Elizabethans as Saturn)   74 *changeable*
i.e., opalescent in effect   78 *nothing* bringing back nothing

DUKE

Let all the rest give place.   79

> *[Exeunt Curio and Attendants.]*
> Once more, Cesario,

Get thee to yond same sovereign cruelty.   80
Tell her, my love, more noble than the world,
Prizes not quantity of dirty lands;
The parts that fortune hath bestowed upon her   83
Tell her I hold as giddily as fortune,
But 'tis that miracle and queen of gems
That nature pranks her in attracts my soul.   86

VIOLA

But if she cannot love you, sir?

DUKE

I cannot be so answered.

VIOLA   Sooth, but you must.
Say that some lady, as perhaps there is,
Hath for your love as great a pang of heart   90
As you have for Olivia. You cannot love her.
You tell her so. Must she not then be answered?

DUKE

There is no woman's sides
Can bide the beating of so strong a passion   94
As love doth give my heart; no woman's heart
So big to hold so much; they lack retention.   96
Alas, their love may be called appetite,
No motion of the liver but the palate,   98
That suffers surfeit, cloyment, and revolt;   99
But mine is all as hungry as the sea   100
And can digest as much. Make no compare
Between that love a woman can bear me
And that I owe Olivia.   103

VIOLA   Ay, but I know –

---

79 *give place* leave 80 *sovereign cruelty* supremely cruel person 83 *parts* possessions 86 *pranks* decks 94 *bide* withstand 96 *retention* capacity of retaining 98 *motion* emotion; *liver* seat of the emotion of love 99 *revolt* revulsion 103 *owe* have toward

DUKE
 What dost thou know?

VIOLA
 Too well what love women to men may owe.
 In faith, they are as true of heart as we.
 My father had a daughter loved a man
 As it might be perhaps, were I a woman,
109 I should your lordship.

DUKE   And what's her history?

VIOLA
110 A blank, my lord. She never told her love,
 But let concealment, like a worm i' th' bud,
112 Feed on her damask cheek. She pined in thought;
 And, with a green and yellow melancholy,
114 She sat like Patience on a monument,
 Smiling at grief. Was not this love indeed?
 We men may say more, swear more; but indeed
117 Our shows are more than will; for still we prove
 Much in our vows but little in our love.

DUKE
 But died thy sister of her love, my boy?

VIOLA
120 I am all the daughters of my father's house,
 And all the brothers too, and yet I know not.
 Sir, shall I to this lady?

DUKE   Ay, that's the theme.
 To her in haste. Give her this jewel. Say
124 My love can give no place, bide no denay.   *Exeunt.*

*

---

109 *history* story 112 *damask* pink and white, as of a damask rose 114 *Patience on a monument* allegorical sculpture of patience 117 *will* our passions 124 *can give no place* cannot yield; *denay* denial

∽ **II.5** *Enter Sir Toby, Sir Andrew, and Fabian.*

TOBY   Come thy ways, Signor Fabian.
FABIAN   Nay, I'll come. If I lose a scruple of this sport, let   2
me be boiled to death with melancholy.   3
TOBY   Wouldst thou not be glad to have the niggardly,   4
rascally sheep-biter come by some notable shame?   5
FABIAN   I would exult, man. You know he brought me
out o' favor with my lady about a bearbaiting here.
TOBY   To anger him we'll have the bear again, and we
will fool him black and blue. Shall we not, Sir Andrew?
ANDREW   An we do not, it is pity of our lives.   10
        Enter Maria.
TOBY   Here comes the little villain. How now, my metal   11
of India?
MARIA   Get ye all three into the boxtree. Malvolio's   13
coming down this walk. He has been yonder i' the sun
practicing behavior to his own shadow this half hour.   15
Observe him, for the love of mockery, for I know this
letter will make a contemplative idiot of him. Close, in   17
the name of jesting. *[The others hide.]* Lie thou there
[Throws down a letter.]; for here comes the trout that
must be caught with tickling.   *Exit.*   20
        Enter Malvolio.
MALVOLIO   'Tis but fortune; all is fortune. Maria once
told me she did affect me; and I have heard herself   22
come thus near, that, should she fancy, it should be one
of my complexion. Besides, she uses me with a more   24
exalted respect than any one else that follows her. What   25
should I think on't?
TOBY   Here's an overweening rogue.

II.5 The garden of Olivia's house   **2** *scruple* bit   **3** *boiled . . . melancholy*
(pun on "bile," the cause of melancholy)   **4** *niggardly* grudging   **5** *sheep-
biter* dog that bites sheep, sneaking fellow   **11–12** *my metal of India* my
golden one   **13** *tree* i.e., hedge   **15** *behavior* elegant conduct   **17** *contemplative idiot* i.e., addled by his musings; *Close* hide   **20** *tickling* stroking
about the gills   **22** *she did affect me* Olivia liked me   **24** *complexion* person-
ality   **25** *that follows her* in her service

FABIAN   O, peace! Contemplation makes a rare turkey
cock of him. How he jets under his advanced plumes!

ANDREW   'Slight, I could so beat the rogue.

TOBY   Peace, I say.

MALVOLIO   To be Count Malvolio.

TOBY   Ah, rogue!

ANDREW   Pistol him, pistol him.

TOBY   Peace, peace.

MALVOLIO   There is example for't. The Lady of the
Strachy married the yeoman of the wardrobe.

ANDREW   Fie on him, Jezebel.

FABIAN   O, peace! Now he's deeply in. Look how imagination blows him.

MALVOLIO   Having been three months married to her,
sitting in my state –

TOBY   O for a stonebow, to hit him in the eye!

MALVOLIO   Calling my officers about me, in my
branched velvet gown; having come from a daybed,
where I have left Olivia sleeping –

TOBY   Fire and brimstone!

FABIAN   O, peace, peace!

MALVOLIO   And then to have the humor of state; and
after a demure travel of regard, telling them I know my
place, as I would they should do theirs, to ask for my
kinsman Toby –

TOBY   Bolts and shackles!

FABIAN   O peace, peace, peace, now, now.

MALVOLIO   Seven of my people, with an obedient start,
make out for him. I frown the while, and perchance
wind up my watch, or play with my – some rich jewel.
Toby approaches; curtsies there to me –

TOBY   Shall this fellow live?

---

29 *jets* struts   30 *'Slight* an oath (by God's light)   36–37 *Lady of the Strachy*
(unidentified allusion)   38 *Jezebel* wicked queen of Israel   40 *blows him*
puffs him up   42 *state* chair of state   43 *stonebow* stone shooter   45
branched embroidered; *daybed* sofa   49 *humor of state* manner and disposition of authority   50 *demure . . . regard* grave survey

FABIAN   Though our silence be drawn from us with cars,   60
yet peace.

MALVOLIO   I extend my hand to him thus, quenching
my familiar smile with an austere regard of control –   63

TOBY   And does not Toby take you a blow o' the lips   64
then?

MALVOLIO   Saying, "Cousin Toby, my fortunes having
cast me on your niece, give me this prerogative of
speech."

TOBY   What, what?

MALVOLIO   "You must amend your drunkenness."   70

TOBY   Out, scab!

FABIAN   Nay, patience, or we break the sinews of our
plot.

MALVOLIO   "Besides, you waste the treasure of your time
with a foolish knight" –

ANDREW   That's me, I warrant you.

MALVOLIO   "One Sir Andrew" –

ANDREW   I knew 'twas I, for many do call me fool.

MALVOLIO   What employment have we here?
   [Takes up the letter.]

FABIAN   Now is the woodcock near the gin.   80

TOBY   O, peace, and the spirit of humors intimate reading aloud to him!

MALVOLIO   By my life, this is my lady's hand. These be
her very C's, her U's, and her T's; and thus makes she   84
her great P's. It is, in contempt of question, her hand.   85

ANDREW   Her C's, her U's, and her T's? Why that?

MALVOLIO   *[Reads.]* "To the unknown beloved, this, and
my good wishes." Her very phrases! By your leave, wax.   88

---

60 *cars* chariots   **63** *regard of control* look of authority   **64** *take* give   **80**
woodcock (a stupid bird); *gin* snare, trap   **84** *C's . . . T's* ("cut" is Elizabethan
slang for women's genitals)   **85** *great P's* capital P's; also pun on her urina-
tion; *in contempt of* beyond   **88** *By . . . wax* (a conventional apology for
breaking a seal)

89   Soft, and the impressure her Lucrece, with which she
90   uses to seal. 'Tis my lady. To whom should this be?

91 FABIAN   This wins him, liver and all.

MALVOLIO   *[Reads.]*

> "Jove knows I love,
>> But who?
> Lips, do not move;
>> No man must know."

96   "No man must know." What follows? The numbers altered! "No man must know." If this should be thee,
Malvolio?

99 TOBY   Marry, hang thee, brock!

MALVOLIO   *[Reads.]*

100
> "I may command where I adore,
>> But silence, like a Lucrece knife,
>> With bloodless stroke my heart doth gore.
>> M. O. A. I. doth sway my life."

104 FABIAN   A fustian riddle.

105 TOBY   Excellent wench, say I.

MALVOLIO   "M. O. A. I. doth sway my life." Nay, but
first, let me see, let me see, let me see.

108 FABIAN   What dish o' poison has she dressed him!

109 TOBY   And with what wing the staniel checks at it!

110 MALVOLIO   "I may command where I adore." Why, she
may command me: I serve her; she is my lady. Why,
112   this is evident to any formal capacity. There is no obstruction in this. And the end; what should that alpha-
betical position portend? If I could make that resemble
something in me! Softly, "M. O. A. I."

116 TOBY   O, ay, make up that. He is now at a cold scent.

---

89 *Soft* careful, slow; *impressure* impression; *Lucrece* chaste Roman heroine
who commits suicide after being raped, pictured on Olivia's seal **91** *liver*
the seat of passion **96** *numbers* meter **99** *Marry* (corruption of "Mary";
mild oath); *brock* badger **104** *fustian* ridiculously elaborate **105** *Excellent
wench* clever girl (Maria) **108** *dressed* prepared **109** *staniel* an inferior
hawk; *checks* turns to pursue the wrong prey **112** *formal* normal **112–13**
obstruction difficulty **116** *cold scent* difficult trail

FABIAN   Sowter will cry upon't for all this, though it be as   117
rank as a fox.

MALVOLIO   M – Malvolio.   M – Why, that begins my
name.   120

FABIAN   Did not I say he would work it out? The cur is
excellent at faults.   122

MALVOLIO   M – But then there is no consonancy in the   123
sequel. That suffers under probation. A should follow,   124
but O does.

FABIAN   And O shall end, I hope.

TOBY   Ay, or I'll cudgel him, and make him cry O.

MALVOLIO   And then I comes behind.

FABIAN   Ay, an you had any eye behind you, you might see
more detraction at your heels than fortunes before you.   130

MALVOLIO   M, O, A, I. This simulation is not as the for-   131
mer; and yet, to crush this a little, it would bow to me,   132
for every one of these letters are in my name. Soft, here
follows prose.

[Reads.] "If this fall into thy hand, revolve. In my stars I   135
am above thee, but be not afraid of greatness. Some are
born great, some achieve greatness, and some have
greatness thrust upon 'em. Thy Fates open their hands;
let thy blood and spirit embrace them; and to inure   139
thyself to what thou art like to be, cast thy humble   140
slough and appear fresh. Be opposite with a kinsman,   141
surly with servants. Let thy tongue tang arguments of   142
state; put thyself into the trick of singularity. She thus   143
advises thee that sighs for thee. Remember who commended thy yellow stockings and wished to see thee
ever cross-gartered. I say, remember. Go to, thou art   146
made, if thou desir'st to be so. If not, let me see thee a

---

117 *Sowter . . . upon't* the hound will pick up the scent   122 *faults* gaps or breaks in the scent   123 *consonancy* agreement   124 *suffers* becomes strained; *probation* testing   131 *simulation* hidden meaning   132 *crush* force   135 *revolve* consider; *stars* fate   139 *inure* accustom   141 *slough* outer skin   142 *tang* sound with   143 *singularity* originality   146 *cross-gartered* wearing hose garters crossed above and below the knee

steward still, the fellow of servants, and not worthy to touch Fortune's fingers. Farewell. She that would alter
150 services with thee,
151   The Fortunate Unhappy."

152 Daylight and champian discovers not more! This is
153 open. I will be proud, I will read politic authors, I will
154 baffle Sir Toby, I will wash off gross acquaintance, I will
155 be point-devise, the very man. I do not now fool my-
156 self, to let imagination jade me, for every reason excites
     to this, that my lady loves me. She did commend my
     yellow stockings of late, she did praise my leg being
     cross-gartered; and in this she manifests herself to my
160 love, and with a kind of injunction drives me to these
161 habits of her liking. I thank my stars, I am happy. I will
162 be strange, stout, in yellow stockings, and cross-
     gartered, even with the swiftness of putting on. Jove
     and my stars be praised. Here is yet a postscript.
     [Reads.] "Thou canst not choose but know who I am. If
166 thou entertain'st my love, let it appear in thy smiling.
     Thy smiles become thee well. Therefore in my presence
     still smile, dear my sweet, I prithee." Jove, I thank thee.
     I will smile; I will do everything that thou wilt have
170 me.   Exit.

FABIAN I will not give my part of this sport for a pension
172 of thousands to be paid from the Sophy.

TOBY I could marry this wench for this device.

ANDREW So could I too.

TOBY And ask no other dowry with her but such another jest.

          Enter Maria.

ANDREW Nor I neither.

---

151 *Unhappy* unfortunate 152 *champian* open country; *discovers* reveals, discloses 153 *politic authors* writers on government 154 *baffle* subject to disgrace 155 *point-devise* perfectly correct 156 *jade* trick 161 *habits* attire 162 *strange* aloof; *stout* proud 166 *entertain'st* accept 172 *Sophy* shah of Persia

FABIAN   Here comes my noble gull-catcher.   178
TOBY   Wilt thou set thy foot o' my neck?
ANDREW   Or o' mine either?   180
TOBY   Shall I play my freedom at tray-trip and become   181
   thy bondslave?
ANDREW   I' faith, or I either?
TOBY   Why, thou hast put him in such a dream that,
   when the image of it leaves him, he must run mad.
MARIA   Nay, but say true, does it work upon him?
TOBY   Like aqua vitae with a midwife.   187
MARIA   If you will, then, see the fruits of the sport, mark
   his first approach before my lady. He will come to her
   in yellow stockings, and 'tis a color she abhors, and   190
   cross-gartered, a fashion she detests; and he will smile
   upon her, which will now be so unsuitable to her disposition, being addicted to a melancholy as she is, that
   it cannot but turn him into a notable contempt. If you
   will see it, follow me.
TOBY   To the gates of Tartar, thou most excellent devil   196
   of wit.
ANDREW   I'll make one too.   *Exeunt.*

                            *

∾ **III.1** *Enter Viola and Clown [with a tabor].*

VIOLA   Save thee, friend, and thy music. Dost thou live   1
   by thy tabor?   2
CLOWN   No, sir, I live by the church.
VIOLA   Art thou a churchman?
CLOWN   No such matter, sir. I do live by the church; for
   I do live at my house, and my house doth stand by the
   church.

---

178 *gull-catcher* fool-catcher   181 *play* gamble; *tray-trip* a game of dice
187 *aqua vitae* any distilled liquor   196 *Tartar* Tartarus, the section of hell
reserved for the most evil
   III.1 Before the house of Olivia   1 *Save thee* God save thee   1–2 *live by*
make a living with   2 *tabor* drum

8   VIOLA   So thou mayst say, the king lies by a beggar, if a
        beggar dwell near him; or, the church stands by thy
10   tabor, if thy tabor stand by the church.
    CLOWN   You have said, sir. To see this age! A sentence is
12   but a chev'ril glove to a good wit. How quickly the
        wrong side may be turned outward!
14 VIOLA   Nay, that's certain. They that dally nicely with
15   words may quickly make them wanton.
    CLOWN   I would therefore my sister had had no name,
        sir.
    VIOLA   Why, man?
    CLOWN   Why, sir, her name's a word, and to dally with
20   that word might make my sister wanton. But indeed
21   words are very rascals since bonds disgraced them.
    VIOLA   Thy reason, man?
    CLOWN   Troth, sir, I can yield you none without words,
        and words are grown so false I am loath to prove reason
        with them.
    VIOLA   I warrant thou art a merry fellow and car'st for
        nothing.
    CLOWN   Not so, sir; I do care for something; but in my
        conscience, sir, I do not care for you. If that be to care
30   for nothing, sir, I would it would make you invisible.
    VIOLA   Art not thou the Lady Olivia's fool?
    CLOWN   No, indeed, sir. The Lady Olivia has no folly.
        She will keep no fool, sir, till she be married; and fools
34   are as like husbands as pilchers are to herrings, the hus-
        band's the bigger. I am indeed not her fool, but her
        corrupter of words.
    VIOLA   I saw thee late at the Count Orsino's.
    CLOWN   Foolery, sir, does walk about the orb like the
        sun; it shines everywhere. I would be sorry, sir, but the

---

8 *lies* dwells, here implying "sleeps with"   12 *chev'ril* kid   14 *dally nicely* play
subtly   15 *wanton* capricious   20 *wanton* abandoned   21 *since . . . them*
i.e., since bonds have been needed to guarantee them   34 *pilchers* pilchards
(small fish resembling herring)

fool should be as oft with your master as with my mis- 40
tress. I think I saw your wisdom there.

VIOLA Nay, an thou pass upon me, I'll no more with 42
thee. Hold, there's expenses for thee.
[Gives a coin.]

CLOWN Now Jove, in his next commodity of hair, send 44
thee a beard.

VIOLA By my troth, I'll tell thee, I am almost sick for
one, though I would not have it grow on my chin. Is
thy lady within?

CLOWN Would not a pair of these have bred, sir?

VIOLA Yes, being kept together and put to use. 50

CLOWN I would play Lord Pandarus of Phrygia, sir, to 51
bring a Cressida to this Troilus.

VIOLA I understand you, sir. 'Tis well begged.
[Gives another coin.]

CLOWN The matter, I hope, is not great, sir, begging but
a beggar: Cressida was a beggar. My lady is within, sir. I 55
will conster to them whence you come. Who you are 56
and what you would are out of my welkin; I might say 57
"element," but the word is overworn. *Exit.*

VIOLA
This fellow is wise enough to play the fool,
And to do that well craves a kind of wit. 60
He must observe their mood on whom he jests,
The quality of persons, and the time;
And like the haggard, check at every feather 63
That comes before his eye. This is a practice 64
As full of labor as a wise man's art;
For folly that he wisely shows, is fit;
But wise men, folly-fall'n, quite taint their wit. 67

---

42 *pass upon* jest at 44 *commodity* shipment 50 *put to use* put out at interest 51 *Pandarus* the go-between in the tale told by Chaucer and others 55
Cressida was a beggar (she became a leprous beggar in Henryson's continua-
tion of Chaucer's story) 56 *conster* construe, explain 57 *welkin* sky 60
wit intelligence 63 *haggard* untrained hawk; *check . . . feather* forsake her
quarry for other game 64 *practice* skill 67 *folly-fall'n* fallen into folly; *taint
their wit* ruin their reputation for intelligence

Enter Sir Toby and [Sir] Andrew.

TOBY   Save you, gentleman.

VIOLA   And you, sir.

70 ANDREW   *Dieu vous garde, monsieur.*

VIOLA   *Et vous aussi; votre serviteur.*

ANDREW   I hope, sir, you are, and I am yours.

73 TOBY   Will you encounter the house? My niece is de-
sirous you should enter, if your trade be to her.

75 VIOLA   I am bound to your niece, sir; I mean, she is the
76 list of my voyage.

77 TOBY   Taste your legs, sir; put them to motion.

78 VIOLA   My legs do better understand me, sir, than I understand what you mean by bidding me taste my legs.

80 TOBY   I mean, to go, sir, to enter.

VIOLA   I will answer you with gait and entrance. But we
82 are prevented.

Enter Olivia and Gentlewoman [Maria].

Most excellent accomplished lady, the heavens rain
odors on you.

ANDREW   That youth's a rare courtier. "Rain odors" –
well!

87 VIOLA   My matter hath no voice, lady, but to your own
88 most pregnant and vouchsafed ear.

ANDREW   "Odors," "pregnant," and "vouchsafed" – I'll
90 get 'em all three all ready.

OLIVIA   Let the garden door be shut, and leave me to my
hearing. *[Exeunt Sir Toby, Sir Andrew, and Maria.]* Give
me your hand, sir.

VIOLA

My duty, madam, and most humble service.

OLIVIA

What is your name?

70–71 *Dieu . . . serviteur* God protect you, sir . . . And you also; your servant
73 *encounter* meet – i.e., go into   75 *bound to* bound for   76 *list* limit, des-
tination   77 *Taste* try   78 *understand* both "comprehend" and "stand
under"   82 *prevented* anticipated   87 *hath no voice* can be told to no one
88 *pregnant* receptive; *vouchsafed* willing

VIOLA
  Cesario is your servant's name, fair princess.
OLIVIA
  My servant, sir? 'Twas never merry world
  Since lowly feigning was called compliment.   98
  You're servant to the Count Orsino, youth.
VIOLA
  And he is yours, and his must needs be yours.   *100*
  Your servant's servant is your servant, madam.
OLIVIA
  For him, I think not on him; for his thoughts,
  Would they were blanks, rather than filled with me.   103
VIOLA
  Madam, I come to whet your gentle thoughts
  On his behalf.
OLIVIA   O, by your leave, I pray you.
  I bade you never speak again of him;
  But, would you undertake another suit,
  I had rather hear you to solicit that
  Than music from the spheres.   109
VIOLA   Dear lady –
OLIVIA
  Give me leave, beseech you. I did send,   *110*
  After the last enchantment you did here,
  A ring in chase of you. So did I abuse   112
  Myself, my servant, and, I fear me, you.
  Under your hard construction must I sit,   114
  To force that on you in a shameful cunning
  Which you knew none of yours. What might you think?
  Have you not set mine honor at the stake
  And baited it with all th' unmuzzled thoughts   118
  That tyrannous heart can think? To one of your receiving   119

---

98 *lowly feigning* false humility   **103** *blanks* blank sheets   **109** *music from the spheres* celestial melody believed to be produced by the several concentric revolving spheres in which the planets and stars were thought to be placed   **112** *abuse* deceive   **114** *construction* interpretation   **118** *baited* harassed, as a chained bear by dogs   **119** *receiving* receptive capacity

120   Enough is shown; a cypress, not a bosom,
     Hides my heart. So, let me hear you speak.

VIOLA
   I pity you.

OLIVIA   That's a degree to love.

VIOLA
123   No, not a grize; for 'tis a vulgar proof
     That very oft we pity enemies.

OLIVIA
   Why then, methinks 'tis time to smile again.
   O world, how apt the poor are to be proud.
   If one should be a prey, how much the better
   To fall before the lion than the wolf.
     Clock strikes.
   The clock upbraids me with the waste of time.
130   Be not afraid, good youth, I will not have you,
     And yet, when wit and youth is come to harvest,
132   Your wife is like to reap a proper man.
     There lies your way, due west.

VIOLA   Then westward ho!
   Grace and good disposition attend your ladyship.
   You'll nothing, madam, to my lord by me?

OLIVIA
   Stay.
   I prithee tell me what thou think'st of me.

VIOLA
   That you do think you are not what you are.

OLIVIA
   If I think so, I think the same of you.

VIOLA
140   Then think you right. I am not what I am.

OLIVIA
   I would you were as I would have you be.

---

120 *cypress* transparent black cloth   123 *grize* grece, flight of steps; *vulgar proof* common experience   132 *proper* handsome

VIOLA
  Would it be better, madam, than I am?
  I wish it might, for now I am your fool.   143

OLIVIA
  O, what a deal of scorn looks beautiful
  In the contempt and anger of his lip.
  A murd'rous guilt shows not itself more soon
  Than love that would seem hid: love's night is noon.
  Cesario, by the roses of the spring,
  By maidhood, honor, truth, and everything,
  I love thee so that, maugre all thy pride,   150
  Nor wit nor reason can my passion hide.
  Do not extort thy reasons from this clause,— *dont jump 2*
  For that I woo, thou therefore hast no cause;   *conclusions*
  But rather reason thus with reason fetter,   154
  Love sought is good, but given unsought is better.

VIOLA
  By innocence I swear, and by my youth,
  I have one heart, one bosom, and one truth,
  And that no woman has; nor never none
  Shall mistress be of it, save I alone.
  And so adieu, good madam. Never more   160
  Will I my master's tears to you deplore.

OLIVIA
  Yet come again; for thou perhaps mayst move
  That heart which now abhors to like his love.   *Exeunt.*

                      *

∾ **III.2** *Enter Sir Toby, Sir Andrew, and Fabian.*

ANDREW No, faith, I'll not stay a jot longer.
TOBY Thy reason, dear venom; give thy reason.   2
FABIAN You must needs yield your reason, Sir Andrew.

---

143 *fool* butt 150 *maugre* despite 154 *reason . . . fetter* bind reason with (stronger) reason
   III.2 Within the house of Olivia 2 *venom* (Sir Andrew is filled with venom)

ANDREW   Marry, I saw your niece do more favors to the
count's servingman than ever she bestowed upon me. I
6   saw't i' th' orchard.

TOBY   Did she see thee the while, old boy? Tell me that.

ANDREW   As plain as I see you now.

9 FABIAN   This was a great argument of love in her toward
10 you.

ANDREW   'Slight! will you make an ass o' me?

12 FABIAN   I will prove it legitimate, sir, upon the oaths of
judgment and reason.

TOBY   And they have been grand-jury men since before
Noah was a sailor.

FABIAN   She did show favor to the youth in your sight
17   only to exasperate you, to awake your dormouse valor,
to put fire in your heart and brimstone in your liver.
You should then have accosted her, and with some ex-
20   cellent jests, fire-new from the mint, you should have
banged the youth into dumbness. This was looked for
22   at your hand, and this was balked. The double gilt of
this opportunity you let time wash off, and you are
24   now sailed into the north of my lady's opinion, where
you will hang like an icicle on a Dutchman's beard unless you do redeem it by some laudable attempt either
of valor or policy.

ANDREW   An't be any way, it must be with valor; for pol-
29   icy I hate. I had as lief be a Brownist as a politician.

30 TOBY   Why then, build me thy fortunes upon the basis
of valor. Challenge me the count's youth to fight with
him; hurt him in eleven places. My niece shall take
note of it, and assure thyself there is no love-broker in
the world can more prevail in man's commendation
with woman than report of valor.

---

6 *orchard* probably "garden"   9 *argument* proof   12 *legitimate* true; *oaths*
testimony   17 *dormouse* i.e., sleepy   22 *balked* missed; *double gilt* twice
dipped in gold   24 *into the north* i.e., out of the warmth   29 *Brownist* early
Congregationalist

FABIAN   There is no way but this, Sir Andrew.

ANDREW   Will either of you bear me a challenge to him?

TOBY   Go, write it in a martial hand. Be curst and brief; 38
it is no matter how witty, so it be eloquent and full of
invention. Taunt him with the license of ink. If thou 40
thou'st him some thrice, it shall not be amiss; and as 41
many lies as will lie in thy sheet of paper, although the
sheet were big enough for the bed of Ware in England, 43
set 'em down. Go about it. Let there be gall enough in
thy ink, though thou write with a goose pen, no matter.
About it!

ANDREW   Where shall I find you?

TOBY   We'll call thee at the cubiculo. Go. 48

Exit Sir Andrew.

FABIAN   This is a dear manikin to you, Sir Toby. 49

TOBY   I have been dear to him, lad, some two thousand 50
strong or so.

FABIAN   We shall have a rare letter from him, but you'll
not deliver't?

TOBY   Never trust me then; and by all means stir on the
youth to an answer. I think oxen and wainropes cannot 55
hale them together. For Andrew, if he were opened, and 56
you find so much blood in his liver as will clog the foot
of a flea, I'll eat the rest of th' anatomy.

FABIAN   And his opposite, the youth, bears in his visage
no great presage of cruelty. 60

Enter Maria.

TOBY   Look where the youngest wren of mine comes. 61

MARIA   If you desire the spleen, and will laugh yourselves 62
into stitches, follow me. Yond gull Malvolio is turned 63
heathen, a very renegado; for there is no Christian that
means to be saved by believing rightly can ever believe

---

38 *curst* perversely cross   40 *license of ink* i.e., with the freedom possible in
writing   41 *thou'st him* call him "thou" instead of the polite "you"   43 *bed
of Ware* a famous bed, over ten feet wide   48 *cubiculo* little chamber   49
manikin puppet   55 *wainropes* wagon ropes   56 *hale* haul   61 *youngest
wren* smallest of small birds   62 *spleen* a laughing fit   63 *gull* dupe

66   such impossible passages of grossness. He's in yellow
     stockings.

TOBY   And cross-gartered?

69   MARIA   Most villainously; like a pedant that keeps a
70   school i' th' church. I have dogged him like his mur-
     derer. He does obey every point of the letter that I
     dropped to betray him. He does smile his face into
73   more lines than is in the new map with the augmenta-
     tion of the Indies. You have not seen such a thing as 'tis.
     I can hardly forbear hurling things at him. I know my
     lady will strike him. If she do, he'll smile, and take't for
     a great favor.

TOBY   Come bring us, bring us where he is.

                                        Exeunt omnes.

                    *

∾ **III.3**   *Enter Sebastian and Antonio.*

SEBASTIAN
     I would not by my will have troubled you;
     But since you make your pleasure of your pains,
     I will no further chide you.

ANTONIO
     I could not stay behind you. My desire
     (More sharp than filèd steel) did spur me forth;
6   And not all love to see you (though so much
     As might have drawn one to a longer voyage)
8   But jealousy what might befall your travel,
9   Being skill-less in these parts; which to a stranger,
10   Unguided and unfriended, often prove
     Rough and unhospitable. My willing love,

---

66 *passages of grossness* statements of exaggerated misinformation **69–70**
like . . . church i.e., like an unfashionable village schoolmaster **73–74**
map . . . Indies (Emerie Molyneux's map, c. 1599, which gave fuller details of
the East Indies and North America, with meridian lines, etc.)

   III.3 A street in the Illyrian capital **6** *not all* not only, not entirely **8**
jealousy solicitude **9** *skill-less in* without knowledge of

The rather by these arguments of fear,
Set forth in your pursuit.
SEBASTIAN   My kind Antonio,
I can no other answer make but thanks,
And thanks, and ever oft good turns
Are shuffled off with such uncurrent pay.   16
But, were my worth as is my conscience firm,   17
You should find better dealing. What's to do?
Shall we go see the relics of this town?   19
ANTONIO
Tomorrow, sir; best first go see your lodging.   20
SEBASTIAN
I am not weary, and 'tis long to night.
I pray you let us satisfy our eyes
With the memorials and the things of fame
That do renown this city.
ANTONIO   Would you'd pardon me.
I do not without danger walk these streets.
Once in a sea fight 'gainst the count his galleys
I did some service; of such note indeed
That, were I ta'en here, it would scarce be answered.   28
SEBASTIAN
Belike you slew great number of his people?
ANTONIO
Th' offense is not of such a bloody nature,   30
Albeit the quality of the time and quarrel
Might well have given us bloody argument.
It might have since been answered in repaying
What we took from them, which for traffic's sake   34
Most of our city did. Only myself stood out;
For which, if I be lapsèd in this place,   36
I shall pay dear.
SEBASTIAN   Do not then walk too open.

---

16 *uncurrent* valueless 17 *worth* wealth; *conscience* right inclination 19
relics monuments 28 *answered* atoned for 34 *traffic's* trade's 36 *lapsèd*
surprised, pounced upon

ANTONIO
    It doth not fit me. Hold, sir, here's my purse.
39   In the south suburbs at the Elephant
40   Is best to lodge. I will bespeak our diet,
    Whiles you beguile the time and feed your knowledge
    With viewing of the town. There shall you have me.

SEBASTIAN
    Why I your purse?

ANTONIO
44   Haply your eye shall light upon some toy
45   You have desire to purchase, and your store
46   I think is not for idle markets, sir.

SEBASTIAN
    I'll be your purse-bearer, and leave you for
    An hour.

ANTONIO   To th' Elephant.

SEBASTIAN   I do remember.   *Exeunt.*

*

❧ **III.4** *Enter Olivia and Maria.*

OLIVIA   *[Aside]*
    I have sent after him; he says he'll come.
2   How shall I feast him? What bestow of him?
    For youth is bought more oft than begged or borrowed.
4   I speak too loud. Where's Malvolio? He is sad and civil,
    And suits well for a servant with my fortunes.
    Where is Malvolio?

MARIA   He's coming, madam, but in very strange man-
8   ner. He is sure possessed, madam.

OLIVIA   Why, what's the matter? Does he rave?

---

39 *the Elephant* an inn   **44** *toy* trifle   **45** *store* store of money   **46** *idle markets* useless purchasings
    III.4 The garden of Olivia's house   **2** *of* on   **4** *sad and civil* serious and sedate   **8** *possessed* mad

MARIA   No, madam, he does nothing but smile. Your   *10*
ladyship were best to have some guard about you if he
come, for sure the man is tainted in's wits.

OLIVIA
Go call him hither. *[Exit Maria.]* I am as mad as he,
If sad and merry madness equal be.
    Enter Malvolio [with Maria].
How now, Malvolio?

MALVOLIO   Sweet lady, ho, ho!

OLIVIA   Smil'st thou? I sent for thee upon a sad occasion.

MALVOLIO   Sad, lady? I could be sad. This does make
some obstruction in the blood, this cross-gartering; but
what of that? If it please the eye of one, it is with me as   *20*
the very true sonnet is, "Please one, and please all."   *21*

OLIVIA   Why, how dost thou, man? What is the matter
with thee?

MALVOLIO   Not black in my mind, though yellow in my
legs. It did come to his hands, and commands shall be
executed. I think we do know the sweet Roman hand.   *26*

OLIVIA   Wilt thou go to bed, Malvolio?

MALVOLIO   To bed? Ay, sweetheart, and I'll come to thee.

OLIVIA   God comfort thee. Why dost thou smile so, and
kiss thy hand so oft?   *30*

MARIA   How do you, Malvolio?

MALVOLIO   At your request? Yes, nightingales answer
daws!   *33*

MARIA   Why appear you with this ridiculous boldness
before my lady?

MALVOLIO   "Be not afraid of greatness." 'Twas well writ.

OLIVIA   What mean'st thou by that, Malvolio?

MALVOLIO   "Some are born great."

OLIVIA   Ha?

MALVOLIO   "Some achieve greatness."   *40*

OLIVIA   What say'st thou?

---

21 *sonnet* any short poem   **26** *Roman hand* Italian style of handwriting   **33**
daws small crows

MALVOLIO "And some have greatness thrust upon them."

OLIVIA Heaven restore thee!

MALVOLIO "Remember who commended thy yellow stockings."

OLIVIA Thy yellow stockings?

MALVOLIO "And wished to see thee cross-gartered."

OLIVIA Cross-gartered?

MALVOLIO "Go to, thou art made, if thou desir'st to be so."

50 OLIVIA Am I made?

MALVOLIO "If not, let me see thee a servant still."

52 OLIVIA Why, this is very midsummer madness.

    Enter Servant.

SERVANT Madam, the young gentleman of the Count Orsino's is returned. I could hardly entreat him back. He attends your ladyship's pleasure.

OLIVIA I'll come to him. *[Exit Servant.]* Good Maria, let this fellow be looked to. Where's my cousin Toby? Let some of my people have a special care of him. I would

59 not have him miscarry for the half of my dowry.

                    Exit [Olivia; then Maria].

60 MALVOLIO O ho, do you come near me now? No worse man than Sir Toby to look to me? This concurs directly with the letter. She sends him on purpose, that I may

63 appear stubborn to him; for she incites me to that in the letter. "Cast thy humble slough," says she; "be opposite with a kinsman, surly with servants; let thy tongue tang with arguments of state; put thyself into the trick of singularity." And consequently sets down the manner how: as, a sad face, a reverend carriage, a slow tongue, in

69 the habit of some sir of note, and so forth. I have limed

70 her; but it is Jove's doing, and Jove make me thankful. And when she went away now, "Let this fellow be

72 looked to." "Fellow." Not "Malvolio," nor after my degree, but "fellow." Why, everything adheres together,

---

52 *midsummer madness* i.e., the height of madness   59 *miscarry* come to harm   63 *stubborn* hard, stiff, rigid   69 *limed* caught   72 *Fellow* companion   72–73 *after my degree* according to my position

that no dram of a scruple, no scruple of a scruple, no 74
obstacle, no incredulous or unsafe circumstance – what 75
can be said? Nothing that can be can come between me
and the full prospect of my hopes. Well, Jove, not I, is
the doer of this, and he is to be thanked.
    Enter [Sir] Toby, Fabian, and Maria.

TOBY Which way is he, in the name of sanctity? If all the
devils of hell be drawn in little, and Legion himself pos- 80
sessed him, yet I'll speak to him.

FABIAN Here he is, here he is! How is't with you, sir?
How is't with you, man?

MALVOLIO Go off; I discard you. Let me enjoy my private. Go off.

MARIA Lo, how hollow the fiend speaks within him! Did
not I tell you? Sir Toby, my lady prays you to have a
care of him.

MALVOLIO Aha! does she so?

TOBY Go to, go to; peace, peace; we must deal gently 90
with him. Let me alone. How do you, Malvolio? How
is't with you? What, man, defy the devil! Consider, he's
an enemy to mankind.

MALVOLIO Do you know what you say?

MARIA La you, an you speak ill of the devil, how he takes
it at heart. Pray God he be not bewitched.

FABIAN Carry his water to th' wise woman. 97

MARIA Marry, and it shall be done tomorrow morning
if I live. My lady would not lose him for more than I'll
say. 100

MALVOLIO How now, mistress?

MARIA O Lord!

TOBY Prithee hold thy peace. This is not the way. Do
you not see you move him? Let me alone with him. 104

---

74 *dram* (1) small bit, (2) one eighth fluid ounce; *scruple* (1) doubt, (2) one
third of a dram   75 *incredulous* incredible   80 *drawn in little* brought together in a small space; *Legion* troop of fiends   97 *water* urine for medical
analysis; *wise woman* herb woman   104 *move* rouse

FABIAN   No way but gentleness; gently, gently. The fiend
is rough and will not be roughly used.

107 TOBY   Why, how now, my bawcock? How dost thou,
108 chuck?

MALVOLIO   Sir!

110 TOBY   Ay, biddy, come with me. What, man, 'tis not for
111 gravity to play at cherry pit with Satan. Hang him, foul
112 collier!

MARIA   Get him to say his prayers; good Sir Toby, get
him to pray.

MALVOLIO   My prayers, minx?

MARIA   No, I warrant you, he will not hear of godliness.

117 MALVOLIO   Go hang yourselves all! You are idle shallow
things; I am not of your element. You shall know more
hereafter.   Exit.

120 TOBY   Is't possible?

FABIAN   If this were played upon a stage now, I could
condemn it as an improbable fiction.

123 TOBY   His very genius hath taken the infection of the device, man.

125 MARIA   Nay, pursue him now, lest the device take air and
taint.

FABIAN   Why, we shall make him mad indeed.

MARIA   The house will be the quieter.

TOBY   Come, we'll have him in a dark room and bound.

130 My niece is already in the belief that he's mad. We may
131 carry it thus, for our pleasure and his penance, till our
very pastime, tired out of breath, prompt us to have
mercy on him; at which time we will bring the device
to the bar and crown thee for a finder of madmen. But
see, but see!

     Enter Sir Andrew.

136 FABIAN   More matter for a May morning.

---

107 *bawcock* fine fellow (French *beau coq*)   108 *chuck* chick   110 *biddy*
chicken   111 *gravity* dignity; *cherry pit* a child's game   112 *collier* coal ped-
dler (Satan)   117 *idle* empty, trifling   123 *genius* nature   125–26 *take air
and taint* be exposed and thus contaminated   131 *carry it* carry the trick on
136 *matter . . . morning* material for a May Day comedy

ANDREW   Here's the challenge; read it. I warrant there's
vinegar and pepper in't.

FABIAN   Is't so saucy?   139

ANDREW   Ay, is't, I warrant him. Do but read.   140

TOBY   Give me. *[Reads.]* "Youth, whatsoever thou art,
thou art but a scurvy fellow."

FABIAN   Good, and valiant.

TOBY   *[Reads.]* "Wonder not nor admire not in thy mind 144
why I do call thee so, for I will show thee no reason
for't."

FABIAN   A good note that keeps you from the blow of the
law.

TOBY   *[Reads.]* "Thou com'st to the Lady Olivia, and in
my sight she uses thee kindly. But thou liest in thy   150
throat; that is not the matter I challenge thee for."

FABIAN   Very brief, and to exceeding good sense – less.

TOBY   *[Reads.]* "I will waylay thee going home; where if
it be thy chance to kill me" –

FABIAN   Good.

TOBY   *[Reads.]* "Thou kill'st me like a rogue and a villain."

FABIAN   Still you keep o' th' windy side of the law. Good.   157

TOBY   *[Reads.]* "Fare thee well, and God have mercy upon
one of our souls. He may have mercy upon mine, but
my hope is better, and so look to thyself. Thy friend, as 160
thou usest him, and thy sworn enemy,

                          Andrew Aguecheek."
If this letter move him not, his legs cannot. I'll give't
him.

MARIA   You may have very fit occasion for't. He is now in
some commerce with my lady and will by and by depart.

TOBY   Go, Sir Andrew. Scout me for him at the corner of
the orchard like a bum-baily. So soon as ever thou seest   169
him, draw; and as thou draw'st, swear horrible; for it   170
comes to pass oft that a terrible oath, with a swaggering

---

139 *saucy* (1) spicy, (2) impudent, sharp   **144** *admire* be amazed   **157**
windy windward, safe   **169** *bum-baily* an agent employed in making arrests

172 accent sharply twanged off, gives manhood more ap-
173 probation than ever proof itself would have earned
     him. Away!
175 ANDREW Nay, let me alone for swearing.   *Exit.*
     TOBY Now will not I deliver his letter; for the behavior
     of the young gentleman gives him out to be of good ca-
     pacity and breeding; his employment between his lord
     and my niece confirms no less. Therefore this letter,
180 being so excellently ignorant, will breed no terror in the
181 youth. He will find it comes from a clodpoll. But, sir, I
     will deliver his challenge by word of mouth, set upon
     Aguecheek a notable report of valor, and drive the gen-
     tleman (as I know his youth will aptly receive it) into a
     most hideous opinion of his rage, skill, fury, and im-
     petuosity. This will so fright them both that they will
187 kill one another by the look, like cockatrices.
          Enter Olivia and Viola.
     FABIAN Here he comes with your niece. Give them way
     till he take leave, and presently after him.
190 TOBY I will meditate the while upon some horrid mes-
     sage for a challenge.
               [Exeunt Sir Toby, Fabian, and Maria.]
     OLIVIA
     I have said too much unto a heart of stone
193 And laid mine honor too unchary on't.
     There's something in me that reproves my fault;
     But such a headstrong potent fault it is
     That it but mocks reproof.
     VIOLA
197 With the same havior that your passion bears
     Goes on my master's griefs.
     OLIVIA
199 Here, wear this jewel for me; 'tis my picture.

172–73 *manhood more approbation* more reputation for courage 173 *proof*
testing 175 *let . . . swearing* leave swearing to me 181 *clodpoll* fool 187
cockatrices basilisks, reptiles able to kill with a glance 193 *unchary on't* care-
lessly on it (the heart of stone) 197 *havior* behavior 199 *jewel* any ornament or trinket; here perhaps "locket"

Refuse it not; it hath no tongue to vex you.   *200*
And I beseech you come again tomorrow.
What shall you ask of me that I'll deny,
That, honor saved, may upon asking give?

VIOLA
Nothing but this: your true love for my master.

OLIVIA
How with mine honor may I give him that
Which I have given to you?

VIOLA   I will acquit you.

OLIVIA
Well, come again tomorrow. Fare thee well.
A fiend like thee might bear my soul to hell.   *[Exit.]* *208*
      Enter [Sir] Toby and Fabian.

TOBY   Gentleman, God save thee.

VIOLA   And you, sir.   *210*

TOBY   That defense thou hast, betake thee to't. Of what
nature the wrongs are thou hast done him, I know not,
but thy intercepter, full of despite, bloody as the   *213*
hunter, attends thee at the orchard end. Dismount thy   *214*
tuck, be yare in thy preparation, for thy assailant is   *215*
quick, skillful, and deadly.

VIOLA   You mistake, sir. I am sure no man hath any quarrel to me. My remembrance is very free and clear from
any image of offense done to any man.

TOBY   You'll find it otherwise, I assure you. Therefore, if *220*
you hold your life at any price, betake you to your
guard; for your opposite hath in him what youth,
strength, skill, and wrath can furnish man withal.

VIOLA   I pray you, sir, what is he?

TOBY   He is knight, dubbed with unhatched rapier and   *225*
on carpet consideration, but he is a devil in private   *226*
brawl. Souls and bodies hath he divorced three; and his
incensement at this moment is so implacable that satis-

---

208 *like thee* in your likeness   **213** *despite* defiance   **214–15** *Dismount thy
tuck* take out your rapier   **215** *yare* quick   **225** *dubbed* knighted; *unhatched*
unhacked   **226** *on carpet consideration* through court favor

faction can be none but by pangs of death and sepul-
230   cher. "Hob, nob" is his word; "give't or take't."

VIOLA   I will return again into the house and desire some
232   conduct of the lady. I am no fighter. I have heard of
some kind of men that put quarrels purposely on oth-
234   ers to taste their valor. Belike this is a man of that quirk.

TOBY   Sir, no. His indignation derives itself out of a very
236   competent injury; therefore get you on and give him
his desire. Back you shall not to the house, unless you
undertake that with me which with as much safety you
might answer him. Therefore on, or strip your sword
240   stark naked; for meddle you must, that's certain, or forswear to wear iron about you.

VIOLA   This is as uncivil as strange. I beseech you do me
this courteous office, as to know of the knight what my
offense to him is. It is something of my negligence,
nothing of my purpose.

TOBY   I will do so. Signor Fabian, stay you by this gentleman till my return.   *Exit.*

VIOLA   Pray you, sir, do you know of this matter?

FABIAN   I know the knight is incensed against you, even
250   to a mortal arbitrament; but nothing of the circumstance more.

VIOLA   I beseech you, what manner of man is he?

FABIAN   Nothing of that wonderful promise, to read him
by his form, as you are like to find him in the proof of
his valor. He is indeed, sir, the most skillful, bloody,
and fatal opposite that you could possibly have found
in any part of Illyria. Will you walk towards him? I will
make your peace with him if I can.

VIOLA   I shall be much bound to you for't. I am one that
260   had rather go with sir priest than sir knight. I care not
who knows so much of my mettle.   *Exeunt.*

---

230 *Hob, nob* have or have not   232 *conduct* protective escort   234 *taste*
test; *quirk* peculiarity   236 *competent* sufficient   240 *meddle* engage (in the
fight)   240–41 *forswear . . . iron* repudiate on oath (your right) to wear a
sword   250 *mortal arbitrament* deadly settlement

Enter [Sir] Toby and [Sir] Andrew.

TOBY   Why, man, he's a very devil; I have not seen such a
firago. I had a pass with him, rapier, scabbard, and all,   263
and he gives me the stuck-in with such a mortal motion   264
that it is inevitable; and on the answer he pays you as   265
surely as your feet hits the ground they step on. They
say he has been fencer to the Sophy.

ANDREW   Pox on't, I'll not meddle with him.   268

TOBY   Ay, but he will not now be pacified. Fabian can
scarce hold him yonder.   270

ANDREW   Plague on't, an I thought he had been valiant,
and so cunning in fence, I'd have seen him damned ere
I'd have challenged him. Let him let the matter slip,
and I'll give him my horse, gray Capilet.

TOBY   I'll make the motion. Stand here; make a good   275
show on't. This shall end without the perdition of souls.   276
[Aside] Marry, I'll ride your horse as well as I ride you.
Enter Fabian and Viola.
I have his horse to take up the quarrel. I have persuaded   278
him the youth's a devil.

FABIAN   He is as horribly conceited of him, and pants   280
and looks pale, as if a bear were at his heels.

TOBY   There's no remedy, sir; he will fight with you for's
oath sake. Marry, he hath better bethought him of his
quarrel, and he finds that now scarce to be worth talk-
ing of. Therefore draw for the supportance of his vow.
He protests he will not hurt you.

VIOLA   *[Aside]* Pray God defend me! A little thing would
make me tell them how much I lack of a man.

FABIAN   Give ground if you see him furious.

TOBY   Come, Sir Andrew, there's no remedy. The gentle-   290
man will for his honor's sake have one bout with you;
he cannot by the duello avoid it; but he has promised   292

---

263 *firago* virago; *pass* bout   264 *stuck-in* thrust, lunge; *motion* action   265 *answer* return   268 *Pox* syphilis   275 *motion* offer   276 *the perdition of souls* i.e., killing   278 *take up* settle   280 *He ... him* he (Cesario) has just as frightening a conception of him (Sir Andrew)   292 *duello* dueling code

me, as he is a gentleman and a soldier, he will not hurt
you. Come on, to't.

ANDREW   Pray God he keep his oath!
    [Draws.]
    Enter Antonio.

VIOLA
    I do assure you 'tis against my will.
    [Draws.]

ANTONIO
    Put up your sword. If this young gentleman
    Have done offense, I take the fault on me;
    If you offend him, I for him defy you.

300 TOBY   You, sir? Why, what are you?

ANTONIO   *[Draws.]*
    One, sir, that for his love dares yet do more
    Than you have heard him brag to you he will.

303 TOBY   Nay, if you be an undertaker, I am for you.
    [Draws.]
    Enter Officers.

FABIAN   O good Sir Toby, hold. Here come the officers.

TOBY   *[To Antonio]* I'll be with you anon.

VIOLA   *[To Sir Andrew]* Pray, sir, put your sword up, if
    you please.

308 ANDREW   Marry, will I, sir; and for that I promised you,
    I'll be as good as my word. He will bear you easily, and
310 reins well.

FIRST OFFICER   This is the man; do thy office.

SECOND OFFICER
    Antonio, I arrest thee at the suit
    Of Count Orsino.

ANTONIO   You do mistake me, sir.

FIRST OFFICER
314 No, sir, no jot. I know your favor well,
    Though now you have no sea cap on your head.
    Take him away. He knows I know him well.

---

303 *undertaker* one who takes up a challenge **308** *that* that which (i.e., the horse) **314** *favor* face

ANTONIO
    I must obey. *[To Viola]* This comes with seeking you.
    But there's no remedy; I shall answer it.
    What will you do, now my necessity
    Makes me to ask you for my purse? It grieves me   *320*
    Much more for what I cannot do for you
    Than what befalls myself. You stand amazed,
    But be of comfort.
SECOND OFFICER   Come, sir, away.
ANTONIO
    I must entreat of you some of that money.
VIOLA
    What money, sir?
    For the fair kindness you have showed me here,
    And part being prompted by your present trouble,
    Out of my lean and low ability
    I'll lend you something. My having is not much.   *330*
    I'll make division of my present with you.   *331*
    Hold, there's half my coffer.   *332*
ANTONIO   Will you deny me now?
    Is't possible that my deserts to you
    Can lack persuasion? Do not tempt my misery,
    Lest that it make me so unsound a man
    As to upbraid you with those kindnesses
    That I have done for you.
VIOLA   I know of none,
    Nor know I you by voice or any feature.
    I hate ingratitude more in a man
    Than lying, vainness, babbling, drunkenness,   *340*
    Or any taint of vice whose strong corruption
    Inhabits our frail blood.
ANTONIO   O heavens themselves!
SECOND OFFICER
    Come, sir, I pray you go.
ANTONIO
    Let me speak a little. This youth that you see here

———
331 *my present* what I have now   **332** *coffer* money

I snatched one half out of the jaws of death;
Relieved him with such sanctity of love,
And to his image, which methought did promise
348   Most venerable worth, did I devotion.

FIRST OFFICER
What's that to us? The time goes by. Away!

ANTONIO
350   But, O, how vile an idol proves this god!
Thou hast, Sebastian, done good feature shame.
In nature there's no blemish but the mind;
353   None can be called deformed but the unkind.
354   Virtue is beauty; but the beauteous evil
355   Are empty trunks, o'erflourished by the devil.

FIRST OFFICER
The man grows mad; away with him! Come, come, sir.

ANTONIO   Lead me on.   *Exit [with Officers].*

VIOLA
Methinks his words do from such passion fly
That he believes himself; so do not I.
360   Prove true, imagination, O, prove true,
That I, dear brother, be now ta'en for you!

TOBY   Come hither, knight; come hither, Fabian. We'll
363   whisper o'er a couplet or two of most sage saws.

VIOLA
He named Sebastian. I my brother know
365   Yet living in my glass. Even such and so
In favor was my brother, and he went
Still in this fashion, color, ornament,
For him I imitate. O, if it prove,
Tempests are kind, and salt waves fresh in love! *[Exit.]*

370   TOBY   A very dishonest paltry boy, and more a coward
than a hare. His dishonesty appears in leaving his

---

348 *venerable* worthy of veneration   353 *unkind* unnatural   354 *beauteous*
fair-seeming   355 *trunks* chests; *o'erflourished* ornamented   363 *sage saws*
wise sayings   365 *Yet . . . glass* i.e., whenever I look in the mirror   370 *dishonest* dishonorable

friend here in necessity and denying him; and for his
cowardship, ask Fabian.

FABIAN   A coward, a most devout coward; religious in it.   374
ANDREW   'Slid, I'll after him again and beat him.
TOBY   Do; cuff him soundly, but never draw thy sword.
ANDREW   An I do not –   *[Exit.]*
FABIAN   Come, let's see the event.   378
TOBY   I dare lay any money 'twill be nothing yet.   379

                                              Exeunt.

                          *

∾ **IV.1** *Enter Sebastian and Clown.*

CLOWN   Will you make me believe that I am not sent for
   you?
SEBASTIAN   Go to, go to, thou art a foolish fellow. Let me
   be clear of thee.
CLOWN   Well held out, i' faith! No, I do not know you;   5
   nor I am not sent to you by my lady, to bid you come
   speak with her; nor your name is not Master Cesario;
   nor this is not my nose neither. Nothing that is so is so.
SEBASTIAN   I prithee vent thy folly somewhere else. Thou
   know'st not me.   10
CLOWN   Vent my folly! He has heard that word of some
   great man, and now applies it to a fool. Vent my folly! I
   am afraid this great lubber, the world, will prove a   13
   cockney. I prithee now, ungird thy strangeness, and tell   14
   me what I shall vent to my lady. Shall I vent to her that
   thou art coming?
SEBASTIAN   I prithee, foolish Greek, depart from me.   17
   There's money for thee. If you tarry longer, I shall give
   worse payment.

---

374 *religious* confirmed   378 *event* result   379 *yet* nevertheless
   IV.1 Before Olivia's house   5 *held out* kept up   13 *lubber* lout   14 *cock-
ney* affected person; *ungird thy strangeness* abandon your strange manner   17
Greek (proverbially "merry" nation)

20 CLOWN By my troth, thou hast an open hand. These
wise men that give fools money get themselves a good
22 report – after fourteen years' purchase.
Enter [Sir] Andrew, [Sir] Toby, and Fabian.
ANDREW Now, sir, have I met you again? There's for
you!
[Strikes Sebastian.]
SEBASTIAN Why, there's for thee, and there, and there!
[Strikes Sir Andrew.]
Are all the people mad?
TOBY Hold, sir, or I'll throw your dagger o'er the house.
[Seizes Sebastian.]
CLOWN This will I tell my lady straight. I would not be
in some of your coats for twopence.   *Exit.*
30 TOBY Come on, sir; hold.
ANDREW Nay, let him alone. I'll go another way to work
32 with him. I'll have an action of battery against him, if
there be any law in Illyria. Though I struck him first,
yet it's no matter for that.
SEBASTIAN Let go thy hand.
TOBY Come, sir, I will not let you go. Come, my young
37 soldier, put up your iron. You are well fleshed. Come on.
SEBASTIAN
I will be free from thee.
[Frees himself.]   What wouldst thou now?
If thou dar'st tempt me further, draw thy sword.
[Draws.]
40 TOBY What, what? Nay then, I must have an ounce or
41 two of this malapert blood from you.
[Draws.]
Enter Olivia.
OLIVIA
Hold, Toby! On thy life I charge thee hold!
TOBY Madam.

---

22 *after ... purchase* i.e., at a high price 32 *action of battery* suit at law for
beating (me) 37 *put up* put away; *well fleshed* made eager by a taste of blood
41 *malapert* impudent

OLIVIA
    Will it be ever thus? Ungracious wretch,
    Fit for the mountains and the barbarous caves,
    Where manners ne'er were preached! Out of my sight!
    Be not offended, dear Cesario.
    Rudesby, be gone.   48
            [Exeunt Sir Toby, Sir Andrew, and Fabian.]
              I prithee, gentle friend,
    Let thy fair wisdom, not thy passion, sway
    In this uncivil and unjust extent   50
    Against thy peace. Go with me to my house,
    And hear thou there how many fruitless pranks
    This ruffian hath botched up, that thou thereby   53
    Mayst smile at this. Thou shalt not choose but go.
    Do not deny. Beshrew his soul for me,   55
    He started one poor heart of mine, in thee.   56
SEBASTIAN
    What relish is in this? How runs the stream?   57
    Or I am mad, or else this is a dream.
    Let fancy still my sense in Lethe steep;   59
    If it be thus to dream, still let me sleep!   60
OLIVIA
    Nay, come, I prithee. Would thou'dst be ruled by me!
SEBASTIAN
    Madam, I will.
OLIVIA   O, say so, and so be.   *Exeunt.*
                   *

---

48 *Rudesby* unmannerly fellow   50 *uncivil* uncivilized; *extent* intrusion   53 *botched up* contrived   55 *Beshrew* curse   56 *started* startled; *heart* (with a pun on "hart")   57 *relish* taste   59 *Lethe* the river of forgetfulness in the underworld

∿ **IV.2** *Enter Maria and Clown.*

MARIA   Nay, I prithee put on this gown and this beard;
2   make him believe thou art Sir Topas the curate. Do it
quickly; I'll call Sir Toby the whilst.   *[Exit.]*
4 CLOWN   Well, I'll put it on, and I will dissemble myself
in't, and I would I were the first that ever dissembled in
6   such a gown. I am not tall enough to become the function well, nor lean enough to be thought a good stu-
8   dent; but to be said an honest man and a good
housekeeper goes as fairly as to say a careful man and a
10   great scholar. The competitors enter.
       Enter [Sir] Toby [and Maria].
TOBY   Jove bless thee, Master Parson.
12 CLOWN   *Bonos dies,* Sir Toby; for, as the old hermit of
Prague, that never saw pen and ink, very wittily said to
14   a niece of King Gorboduc, "That that is is"; so, I, being
Master Parson, am Master Parson; for what is "that"
but that, and "is" but is?
TOBY   To him, Sir Topas.
CLOWN   What ho, I say. Peace in this prison!
19 TOBY   The knave counterfeits well; a good knave.
       Malvolio within.
20 MALVOLIO   Who calls there?
CLOWN   Sir Topas the curate, who comes to visit Malvolio the lunatic.
MALVOLIO   Sir Topas, Sir Topas, good Sir Topas, go to
my lady.
25 CLOWN   Out, hyperbolical fiend! How vexest thou this
man! Talkest thou nothing but of ladies?
TOBY   Well said, Master Parson.

IV.2 *Within Olivia's house*   2 *Sir* (common title of address for the clergy);
Topas comic knight in Chaucer (the topaz stone was thought to cure insanity)   4 *dissemble* disguise   6–7 *function* function of a cleric   8–9 *good
housekeeper* householder, neighbor   10 *competitors* associates   12 *Bonos dies*
good day   12–13 *the old hermit of Prague* (probably the clown's invention)
14 *King Gorboduc* a legendary British king who appeared in an early English
tragedy   19 *knave* boy, fellow   25 *hyperbolical* enormous

MALVOLIO Sir Topas, never was man thus wronged.
Good Sir Topas, do not think I am mad. They have laid
me here in hideous darkness.   30

CLOWN Fie, thou dishonest Satan! I call thee by the   31
most modest terms, for I am one of those gentle ones
that will use the devil himself with courtesy. Say'st thou
that house is dark?   34

MALVOLIO As hell, Sir Topas.

CLOWN Why, it hath bay windows transparent as barri-   36
cadoes, and the clerestories toward the south north are   37
as lustrous as ebony; and yet complainest thou of obstruction?

MALVOLIO I am not mad, Sir Topas. I say to you this   40
house is dark.

CLOWN Madman, thou errest. I say there is no darkness
but ignorance, in which thou art more puzzled than the
Egyptians in their fog.   44

MALVOLIO I say this house is as dark as ignorance,
though ignorance were as dark as hell; and I say there
was never man thus abused. I am no more mad than
you are. Make the trial of it in any constant question.   48

CLOWN What is the opinion of Pythagoras concerning   49
wildfowl?   50

MALVOLIO That the soul of our grandam might happily   51
inhabit a bird.

CLOWN What think'st thou of his opinion?

MALVOLIO I think nobly of the soul and no way approve
his opinion.

CLOWN Fare thee well. Remain thou still in darkness.
Thou shalt hold th' opinion of Pythagoras ere I will
allow of thy wits, and fear to kill a woodcock, lest thou   58
dispossess the soul of thy grandam. Fare thee well.

MALVOLIO Sir Topas, Sir Topas!   60

---

31 *dishonest* dishonorable 34 *house* i.e., room 36–37 *barricadoes* barri-
cades 37 *clerestories* upper windows 44 *fog* (Moses brought a three-day fog
on the Egyptians) 48 *constant question* consistent discussion 49 *Pythagoras* (who originated the doctrine of transmigration of souls) 51 *happily*
haply, by chance 58 *allow of* acknowledge

TOBY   My most exquisite Sir Topas!

62 CLOWN   Nay, I am for all waters.

MARIA   Thou mightest have done this without thy beard
and gown. He sees thee not.

TOBY   To him in thine own voice, and bring me word
how thou find'st him. *[To Maria]* I would we were well
rid of this knavery. If he may be conveniently delivered,
I would he were; for I am now so far in offense with my
niece that I cannot pursue with any safety this sport to
70   the upshot. *[To the Clown]* Come by and by to my
chamber.   *Exit [with Maria].*

CLOWN   *[Sings.]*
72   "Hey, Robin, jolly Robin,
               Tell me how thy lady does."

MALVOLIO   Fool.

75 CLOWN   "My lady is unkind, perdie!"

MALVOLIO   Fool.

CLOWN   "Alas, why is she so?"

MALVOLIO   Fool, I say.

CLOWN   "She loves another." Who calls, ha?

80 MALVOLIO   Good fool, as ever thou wilt deserve well at
my hand, help me to a candle, and pen, ink, and paper.
As I am a gentleman, I will live to be thankful to thee
for't.

CLOWN   Master Malvolio?

MALVOLIO   Ay, good fool.

86 CLOWN   Alas, sir, how fell you besides your five wits?

MALVOLIO   Fool, there was never man so notoriously
abused. I am as well in my wits, fool, as thou art.

CLOWN   But as well? Then you are mad indeed, if you be
90   no better in your wits than a fool.

---

62 *for all waters* i.e., good for any trade   70 *upshot* outcome   72–73 *Hey,
Robin . . .* (from an old song, sometimes attributed to Sir Thomas Wyatt)
75 *perdie* certainly   86 *besides your five wits* out of your mind

MALVOLIO   They have here propertied me; keep me in   91
   darkness, send ministers to me, asses, and do all they
   can to face me out of my wits.   93
CLOWN   Advise you what you say. The minister is here. –   94
   Malvolio, Malvolio, thy wits the heavens restore. En-
   deavor thyself to sleep and leave thy vain bibble-babble.
MALVOLIO   Sir Topas.
CLOWN   Maintain no words with him, good fellow. –
   Who, I, sir? Not I, sir. God b' wi' you, good Sir
   Topas. – Marry, amen. – I will, sir, I will.   100
MALVOLIO   Fool, fool, fool, I say!
CLOWN   Alas, sir, be patient. What say you, sir? I am
   shent for speaking to you.   103
MALVOLIO   Good fool, help me to some light and some
   paper. I tell thee, I am as well in my wits as any man in
   Illyria.
CLOWN   Welladay that you were, sir.   107
MALVOLIO   By this hand, I am. Good fool, some ink,
   paper, and light; and convey what I will set down to my
   lady. It shall advantage thee more than ever the bearing   110
   of letter did.
CLOWN   I will help you to't. But tell me true, are you not
   mad indeed? or do you but counterfeit?
MALVOLIO   Believe me, I am not. I tell thee true.
CLOWN   Nay, I'll ne'er believe a madman till I see his
   brains. I will fetch you light and paper and ink.
MALVOLIO   Fool, I'll requite it in the highest degree. I
   prithee be gone.
CLOWN   *[Sings.]*

          I am gone, sir,
          And anon, sir,   120
       I'll be with you again,
          In a trice,
          Like to the old Vice,   123

---

91 *propertied me* made me a property, a mere thing   **93** *face me* brazen me
94 *Advise you* be careful   **103** *shent* reproved   **107** *Welladay* woe, alas   **123**
Vice comic character in old morality plays

Your need to sustain.

125   Who with dagger of lath,
In his rage and his wrath,

127   Cries "Ah ha" to the devil.
Like a mad lad,
"Pare thy nails, dad."

130   Adieu, goodman devil.   *Exit.*

*

~ **IV.3** *Enter Sebastian.*

SEBASTIAN
This is the air; that is the glorious sun;
This pearl she gave me, I do feel't and see't;
And though 'tis wonder that enwraps me thus,
Yet 'tis not madness. Where's Antonio then?
I could not find him at the Elephant;

6   Yet there he was, and there I found this credit,
That he did range the town to seek me out.
His counsel now might do me golden service;
For though my soul disputes well with my sense

10   That this may be some error, but no madness,
Yet doth this accident and flood of fortune

12   So far exceed all instance, all discourse,
That I am ready to distrust mine eyes

14   And wrangle with my reason that persuades me
To any other trust but that I am mad,
Or else the lady's mad. Yet, if 'twere so,

17   She could not sway her house, command her followers,

18   Take and give back affairs and their dispatch
With such a smooth, discreet, and stable bearing

20   As I perceive she does. There's something in't

21   That is deceivable. But here the lady comes.

---

125 *lath* wood (i.e., stage dagger)   127–29 (Vice defies his "father," Satan, in those terms)

   IV.3 The house of Olivia   6 *was* had been; *credit* belief   12 *instance* example; *discourse* logic   14 *wrangle* dispute   17 *sway* rule   18 *dispatch* management   21 *deceivable* deceptive

Enter Olivia and Priest.

OLIVIA

Blame not this haste of mine. If you mean well,
Now go with me and with this holy man
Into the chantry by. There, before him,   24
And underneath that consecrated roof,
Plight me the full assurance of your faith,
That my most jealous and too doubtful soul   27
May live at peace. He shall conceal it
Whiles you are willing it shall come to note,   29
What time we will our celebration keep   30
According to my birth. What do you say?

SEBASTIAN

I'll follow this good man and go with you
And having sworn truth, ever will be true.

OLIVIA

Then lead the way, good father, and heavens so shine
That they may fairly note this act of mine.   *Exeunt.*

＊

∾ **V.1** *Enter Clown and Fabian.*

FABIAN   Now as thou lov'st me, let me see his letter.
CLOWN   Good Master Fabian, grant me another request.
FABIAN   Anything.
CLOWN   Do not desire to see this letter.
FABIAN   This is to give a dog, and in recompense desire
my dog again.
     Enter Duke, Viola, Curio, and Lords.
DUKE   Belong you to the Lady Olivia, friends?   7
CLOWN   Ay, sir, we are some of her trappings.
DUKE   I know thee well. How dost thou, my good fel-
low?   10
CLOWN   Truly, sir, the better for my foes, and the worse
for my friends.

———
24 *chantry by* chapel nearby   27 *jealous* anxious   29 *Whiles* until
    V.1 Before Olivia's house   7 *Belong you* i.e., are you in the service of

DUKE   Just the contrary: the better for thy friends.

CLOWN   No, sir, the worse.

DUKE   How can that be?

CLOWN   Marry, sir, they praise me and make an ass of me. Now my foes tell me plainly I am an ass; so that by my foes, sir, I profit in the knowledge of myself, and by

19   my friends I am abused; so that, conclusions to be as

20   kisses, if your four negatives make your two affirmatives, why then, the worse for my friends, and the better for my foes.

DUKE   Why, this is excellent.

CLOWN   By my troth, sir, no, though it please you to be one of my friends.

DUKE   Thou shalt not be the worse for me. There's gold.

27   CLOWN   But that it would be double-dealing, sir, I would you could make it another.

DUKE   O, you give me ill counsel.

30   CLOWN   Put your grace in your pocket, sir, for this once, and let your flesh and blood obey it.

DUKE   Well, I will be so much a sinner to be a double-dealer. There's another.

34   CLOWN   *Primo, secundo, tertio* is a good play; and the old

35   saying is "The third pays for all." The triplex, sir, is a

36   good tripping measure; or the bells of Saint Bennet, sir, may put you in mind – one, two, three.

DUKE   You can fool no more money out of me at this

39   throw. If you will let your lady know I am here to speak

40   with her, and bring her along with you, it may awake my bounty further.

CLOWN   Marry, sir, lullaby to your bounty. Till I come again, I go, sir; but I would not have you to think that my desire of having is the sin of covetousness. But, as

---

19 *abused* deceived   **19–20** *conclusions . . . kisses* with conclusions as with kisses (i.e., the same rule applies)   **27** *double-dealing* (1) double giving, (2) deceit   **30** *your grace* (1) title of address, (2) your generosity   **34** *play* (probably a children's game)   **35** *triplex* triple time in music   **36** *Saint Bennet* Saint Benedict's church   **39** *throw* throw of the dice

you say, sir, let your bounty take a nap; I will awake it
anon.   *Exit.*
    Enter Antonio and Officers.

VIOLA
    Here comes the man, sir, that did rescue me.

DUKE
    That face of his I do remember well;
    Yet when I saw it last, it was besmeared
    As black as Vulcan in the smoke of war.   50
    A baubling vessel was he captain of,   51
    For shallow draft and bulk unprizable,   52
    With which such scathful grapple did he make   53
    With the most noble bottom of our fleet   54
    That very envy and the tongue of loss   55
    Cried fame and honor on him. What's the matter?

FIRST OFFICER
    Orsino, this is that Antonio
    That took the *Phoenix* and her fraught from Candy;   58
    And this is he that did the *Tiger* board
    When your young nephew Titus lost his leg.   60
    Here in the streets, desperate of shame and state,   61
    In private brabble did we apprehend him.   62

VIOLA
    He did me kindness, sir; drew on my side;
    But in conclusion put strange speech upon me.
    I know not what 'twas but distraction.   65

DUKE
    Notable pirate, thou saltwater thief,
    What foolish boldness brought thee to their mercies
    Whom thou in terms so bloody and so dear   68
    Hast made thine enemies?

---

50 *Vulcan* Roman blacksmith god of fire and patron of metalworkers 51
baubling trifling 52 *unprizable* unworthy of being taken as a prize 53
scathful harmful 54 *bottom* ship 55 *very envy* even malice; *loss* the losers
58 *fraught* cargo; *Candy* Candia (Crete) 61 *desperate* reckless 62 *brabble*
brawl 65 *distraction* madness 68 *dear* costly

ANTONIO   Orsino, noble sir,

70   Be pleased that I shake off these names you give me.
Antonio never yet was thief or pirate,

72   Though I confess, on base and ground enough,
Orsino's enemy. A witchcraft drew me hither.
That most ingrateful boy there by your side
From the rude sea's enraged and foamy mouth
Did I redeem. A wrack past hope he was.
His life I gave him, and did thereto add
My love without retention or restraint,
All his in dedication. For his sake

80   Did I expose myself (pure for his love)
Into the danger of this adverse town;
Drew to defend him when he was beset;
Where being apprehended, his false cunning
(Not meaning to partake with me in danger)

85   Taught him to face me out of his acquaintance,

86   And grew a twenty years removèd thing
While one would wink; denied me mine own purse,

88   Which I had recommended to his use
Not half an hour before.

VIOLA   How can this be?

DUKE

90   When came he to this town?

ANTONIO

Today, my lord; and for three months before,
No int'rim, not a minute's vacancy,
Both day and night did we keep company.
Enter Olivia and Attendants.

DUKE

Here comes the countess; now heaven walks on earth.
But for thee, fellow: fellow, thy words are madness.
Three months this youth hath tended upon me;
But more of that anon. Take him aside.

---

72 *base and ground* solid grounds   80 *pure* purely   85 *face . . . acquaintance*
pretend not to know me   86 *removèd* estranged   88 *recommended* entrusted

OLIVIA
   What would my lord, but that he may not have,   98
   Wherein Olivia may seem serviceable?
   Cesario, you do not keep promise with me.   *100*
VIOLA
   Madam?
DUKE
   Gracious Olivia –
OLIVIA
   What do you say, Cesario? – Good my lord –
VIOLA
   My lord would speak; my duty hushes me.
OLIVIA
   If it be aught to the old tune, my lord,
   It is as fat and fulsome to mine ear   106
   As howling after music.
DUKE   Still so cruel?
OLIVIA
   Still so constant, lord.
DUKE
   What, to perverseness? You uncivil lady,
   To whose ingrate and unauspicious altars   *110*
   My soul the faithfull'st off'rings have breathed out
   That e'er devotion tendered. What shall I do?
OLIVIA
   Even what it please my lord, that shall become him.
DUKE
   Why should I not, had I the heart to do it,
   Like to th' Egyptian thief at point of death   115
   Kill what I love? (A savage jealousy
   That sometimes savors nobly.) But hear me this:
   Since you to non-regardance cast my faith,   118
   And that I partly know the instrument
   That screws me from my true place in your favor,   *120*

---

98 *but that* except what **106** *fat* superfluous; *fulsome* offensive **115** *th' Egyptian thief* Thyamis in the *Aethiopica*, a Greek prose romance by Heliodorus **118** *non-regardance* neglect **120** *screws* pries

Live you the marble-breasted tyrant still.

122 But this your minion, whom I know you love,

123 And whom, by heaven I swear, I tender dearly,

Him will I tear out of that cruel eye

125 Where he sits crownèd in his master's spite.

Come, boy, with me. My thoughts are ripe in mischief.

I'll sacrifice the lamb that I do love

To spite a raven's heart within a dove.   *[Going]*

VIOLA

129 And I, most jocund, apt, and willingly,

130 To do you rest a thousand deaths would die.

[Following]

OLIVIA

Where goes Cesario?

VIOLA   After him I love

More than I love these eyes, more than my life,

133 More, by all mores, than e'er I shall love wife.

If I do feign, you witnesses above

Punish my life for tainting of my love!

OLIVIA

Ay me detested! How am I beguiled!

VIOLA

Who does beguile you? Who does do you wrong?

OLIVIA

Hast thou forgot thyself? Is it so long?

Call forth the holy father.   *[Exit an Attendant.]*

DUKE   *[To Viola]*   Come, away!

OLIVIA

140 Whither, my lord? Cesario, husband, stay.

DUKE

Husband?

OLIVIA   Ay, husband. Can he that deny?

DUKE

Her husband, sirrah?

---

122 *minion* favorite   123 *tender* hold   125 *in . . . spite* despite his master
129 *apt* properly   130 *do you rest* give you peace   133 *all mores* i.e., all conceivable comparisons

VIOLA   No, my lord, not I.
OLIVIA
  Alas, it is the baseness of thy fear
  That makes thee strangle thy propriety.   144
  Fear not, Cesario; take thy fortunes up;
  Be that thou know'st thou art, and then thou art
  As great as that thou fear'st.   147
    Enter Priest.

                          O, welcome, father!
  Father, I charge thee by thy reverence
  Here to unfold – though lately we intended
  To keep in darkness what occasion now   *150*
  Reveals before 'tis ripe – what thou dost know
  Hath newly passed between this youth and me.
PRIEST
  A contract of eternal bond of love,
  Confirmed by mutual joinder of your hands,
  Attested by the holy close of lips,   155
  Strengthened by interchangement of your rings;
  And all the ceremony of this compact
  Sealed in my function, by my testimony;
  Since when, my watch hath told me, toward my grave
  I have traveled but two hours.   *160*
DUKE
  O thou dissembling cub, what wilt thou be
  When time hath sowed a grizzle on thy case?   162
  Or will not else thy craft so quickly grow
  That thine own trip shall be thine overthrow?   164
  Farewell, and take her; but direct thy feet
  Where thou and I, henceforth, may never meet.
VIOLA
  My lord, I do protest –
OLIVIA   O, do not swear.
  Hold little faith, though thou hast too much fear.   168

---

144 *strangle thy propriety* deny who and what you are   147 *that thou fear'st*
i.e., the duke   155 *close* meeting   162 *a grizzle* gray hair; *case* sheath – i.e.,
skin   164 *trip* trickery   168 *little* a little

Enter Sir Andrew.

ANDREW   For the love of God, a surgeon! Send one
170   presently to Sir Toby.

OLIVIA   What's the matter?

172 ANDREW   Has broke my head across, and has given Sir
    Toby a bloody coxcomb too. For the love of God, your
    help! I had rather than forty pounds I were at home.

OLIVIA   Who has done this, Sir Andrew?

ANDREW   The count's gentleman, one Cesario. We took
177   him for a coward, but he's the very devil incardinate.

DUKE   My gentleman Cesario?

179 ANDREW   Od's lifelings, here he is! You broke my head
180   for nothing; and that that I did, I was set on to do't by
    Sir Toby.

VIOLA
    Why do you speak to me? I never hurt you.
    You drew your sword upon me without cause,
    But I bespake you fair and hurt you not.
        Enter [Sir] Toby and Clown.

ANDREW   If a bloody coxcomb be a hurt, you have hurt
    me. I think you set nothing by a bloody coxcomb. Here
187   comes Sir Toby halting; you shall hear more. But if he
188   had not been in drink, he would have tickled you oth-
    ergates than he did.

190 DUKE   How now, gentleman? How is't with you?

TOBY   That's all one! Has hurt me, and there's th' end
    on't. Sot, didst see Dick Surgeon, sot?

CLOWN   O, he's drunk, Sir Toby, an hour agone. His eyes
194   were set at eight i' th' morning.

195 TOBY   Then he's a rogue and a passy measures pavin. I
    hate a drunken rogue.

OLIVIA   Away with him! Who hath made this havoc with
    them?

---

170 *presently* at once   **172** *Has* he has   **177** *incardinate* incarnate   **179** *Od's
lifelings* by God's little life   **187** *halting* limping   **188–89** *othergates* otherwise   **194** *set* fixed or gone down 3

ANDREW I'll help you, Sir Toby, because we'll be dressed
   together.   *200*
TOBY Will you help? An ass-head and a coxcomb and a
   knave, a thin-faced knave, a gull?
OLIVIA Get him to bed, and let his hurt be looked to.
   [Exeunt Clown, Fabian, Sir Toby, and Sir Andrew.]
   Enter Sebastian.

SEBASTIAN
  I am sorry, madam, I have hurt your kinsman;
  But had it been the brother of my blood,
  I must have done no less with wit and safety.   *206*
  You throw a strange regard upon me, and by that   *207*
  I do perceive it hath offended you.
  Pardon me, sweet one, even for the vows
  We made each other but so late ago.   *210*

DUKE
  One face, one voice, one habit, and two persons –   *211*
  A natural perspective that is and is not.   *212*

SEBASTIAN
  Antonio, O my dear Antonio,
  How have the hours racked and tortured me
  Since I have lost thee!

ANTONIO
  Sebastian are you?

SEBASTIAN   Fear'st thou that, Antonio?

ANTONIO
  How have you made division of yourself?
  An apple cleft in two is not more twin
  Than these two creatures. Which is Sebastian?

OLIVIA
  Most wonderful.   *220*

SEBASTIAN
  Do I stand there? I never had a brother;
  Nor can there be that deity in my nature

---

206 *wit and safety* intelligent regard for my safety **207** *strange regard* estranged look **211** *habit* dress **212** *perspective* glass producing an optical illusion

Of here and everywhere. I had a sister,
Whom the blind waves and surges have devoured.
Of charity, what kin are you to me?
What countryman? What name? What parentage?

VIOLA
Of Messaline; Sebastian was my father;
Such a Sebastian was my brother too;

229 So went he suited to his watery tomb.

230 If spirits can assume both form and suit,
You come to fright us.

SEBASTIAN   A spirit I am indeed,

232 But am in that dimension grossly clad

233 Which from the womb I did participate.

234 Were you a woman, as the rest goes even,
I should my tears let fall upon your cheek
And say, "Thrice welcome, drownèd Viola!"

VIOLA
My father had a mole upon his brow.

SEBASTIAN
And so had mine.

VIOLA
And died that day when Viola from her birth

240 Had numbered thirteen years.

SEBASTIAN
241 O, that record is lively in my soul!
He finishèd indeed his mortal act
That day that made my sister thirteen years.

VIOLA
244 If nothing lets to make us happy both
But this my masculine usurped attire,
Do not embrace me till each circumstance

247 Of place, time, fortune do cohere and jump
That I am Viola; which to confirm,
I'll bring you to a captain in this town,

---

229 *suited* dressed   232 *dimension* form; *grossly* in the flesh   233 *participate*
inherit   234 *rest goes even* other circumstances allow   241 *record* memory
244 *lets* hinders   247 *jump* agree completely

Where lie my maiden weeds; by whose gentle help   250
I was preserved to serve this noble count.
All the occurrence of my fortune since
Hath been between this lady and this lord.

SEBASTIAN   *[To Olivia]*
So comes it, lady, you have been mistook.
But nature to her bias drew in that.   255
You would have been contracted to a maid;
Nor are you therein, by my life, deceived:
You are betrothed both to a maid and man.

DUKE
Be not amazed; right noble is his blood.
If this be so, as yet the glass seems true,   260
I shall have share in this most happy wrack.
     [To Viola]
Boy, thou hast said to me a thousand times
Thou never shouldst love woman like to me.

VIOLA
And all those sayings will I over swear,   264
And all those swearings keep as true in soul
As doth that orbèd continent the fire   266
That severs day from night.

DUKE   Give me thy hand,
And let me see thee in thy woman's weeds.

VIOLA
The captain that did bring me first on shore
Hath my maid's garments. He upon some action   270
Is now in durance, at Malvolio's suit,   271
A gentleman, and follower of my lady's.

OLIVIA
He shall enlarge him. Fetch Malvolio hither.   273
And yet alas, now I remember me,
They say, poor gentleman, he's much distract.

---

250 *weeds* clothes   255 *to her bias drew* i.e., drew you into a natural course
(from bowls, in which a weighted ball follows a curved path to its object)
260 *glass* perspective glass   264 *over swear* swear over again   266 *orbèd
continent* sphere of the sun   270 *action* legal charge   271 *durance* custody
273 *enlarge* free

Enter Clown with a letter, and Fabian.

276   A most extracting frenzy of mine own
From my remembrance clearly banished his.
How does he, sirrah?

279   CLOWN   Truly, madam, he holds Belzebub at the stave's
280   end as well as a man in his case may do. Has here writ a
letter to you; I should have given't you today morning.
282   But as a madman's epistles are no gospels, so it skills not
much when they are delivered.

OLIVIA   Open't and read it.

285   CLOWN   Look then to be well edified, when the fool delivers the madman. *[Reads in a loud voice.]* "By the
Lord, madam" –

OLIVIA   How now? Art thou mad?

CLOWN   No, madam, I do but read madness. An your
290   ladyship will have it as it ought to be, you must allow
291   *vox.*

OLIVIA   Prithee read i' thy right wits.

CLOWN   So I do, madonna; but to read his right wits is to
294   read thus. Therefore perpend, my princess, and give ear.

OLIVIA   *[To Fabian]* Read it you, sirrah.

FABIAN   *[Reads.]* "By the Lord, madam, you wrong me,
and the world shall know it. Though you have put me
into darkness, and given your drunken cousin rule over
me, yet have I the benefit of my senses as well as your
300   ladyship. I have your own letter that induced me to the
semblance I put on; with the which I doubt not but to
do myself much right, or you much shame. Think of
me as you please. I leave my duty a little unthought of,
and speak out of my injury.

                                The madly used Malvolio."

OLIVIA   Did he write this?

CLOWN   Ay, madam.

308   DUKE   This savors not much of distraction.

---

276 *extracting* distracting   279–80 *holds . . . end* i.e., holds the devil off with
a long staff   282 *skills* matters   285–86 *delivers* speaks the words of   291
vox amplification   294 *perpend* consider   308 *distraction* insanity

OLIVIA
  See him delivered, Fabian; bring him hither.

                              [Exit Fabian.]

  My lord, so please you, these things further thought on,   *310*
  To think me as well a sister as a wife,
  One day shall crown th' alliance on't, so please you,
  Here at my house and at my proper cost.   *313*

DUKE
  Madam, I am most apt t' embrace your offer.   *314*
    [To Viola]
  Your master quits you; and for your service done him,   *315*
  So much against the mettle of your sex,
  So far beneath your soft and tender breeding,
  And since you called me master for so long,
  Here is my hand; you shall from this time be
  Your master's mistress.   *320*

OLIVIA   A sister; you are she.
    Enter [Fabian, with] Malvolio.

DUKE
  Is this the madman?

OLIVIA   Ay, my lord, this same.
  How now, Malvolio?

MALVOLIO   Madam, you have done me wrong,
  Notorious wrong.   *323*

OLIVIA   Have I, Malvolio? No.

MALVOLIO
  Lady, you have. Pray you peruse that letter.
  You must not now deny it is your hand.
  Write from it if you can, in hand or phrase,   *326*
  Or say 'tis not your seal, not your invention.   *327*
  You can say none of this. Well, grant it then,
  And tell me, in the modesty of honor,   *329*
  Why you have given me such clear lights of favor,   *330*
  Bade me come smiling and cross-gartered to you,

---

313 *proper* own 314 *apt* ready 315 *quits* releases 323 *Notorious* scandalous 326 *from it* differently 327 *invention* composition 329 *in . . . honor* with honorable propriety

To put on yellow stockings, and to frown
333   Upon Sir Toby and the lighter people;
And, acting this in an obedient hope,
Why have you suffered me to be imprisoned,
Kept in a dark house, visited by the priest,
337   And made the most notorious geck and gull
That e'er invention played on? Tell me why.

OLIVIA
Alas, Malvolio, this is not my writing,
340   Though I confess much like the character;
But, out of question, 'tis Maria's hand.
And now I do bethink me, it was she
First told me thou wast mad. Thou cam'st in smiling,
344   And in such forms which here were presupposed
Upon thee in the letter. Prithee be content.
346   This practice hath most shrewdly passed upon thee;
But when we know the grounds and authors of it,
Thou shalt be both the plaintiff and the judge
Of thine own cause.

FABIAN   Good madam, hear me speak,
350   And let no quarrel, nor no brawl to come,
Taint the condition of this present hour,
Which I have wondered at. In hope it shall not.
Most freely I confess myself and Toby
Set this device against Malvolio here,
355   Upon some stubborn and uncourteous parts
We had conceived against him. Maria writ
357   The letter, at Sir Toby's great importance,
In recompense whereof he hath married her.
How with a sportful malice it was followed
360   May rather pluck on laughter than revenge,
If that the injuries be justly weighed
That have on both sides passed.

---

333 *lighter* lesser   337 *geck and gull* ludicrous dupe   340 *character* handwriting   344–45 *presupposed/Upon thee* put upon you beforehand   346 *shrewdly passed* maliciously been put   355 *Upon* on account of   357 *importance* importunity

OLIVIA

  Alas, poor fool, how have they baffled thee!   363

CLOWN   Why, "some are born great, some achieve greatness, and some have greatness thrown upon them." I
was one, sir, in this interlude, one Sir Topas, sir; but 366
that's all one. "By the Lord, fool, I am not mad!" But
do you remember, "Madam, why laugh you at such a
barren rascal? An you smile not, he's gagged"? And thus
the whirligig of time brings in his revenges.   370

MALVOLIO   I'll be revenged on the whole pack of you!

                                    [Exit.]

OLIVIA

  He hath been most notoriously abused.

DUKE

  Pursue him and entreat him to a peace.
  He hath not told us of the captain yet.
  When that is known, and golden time convents,   375
  A solemn combination shall be made
  Of our dear souls. Meantime, sweet sister,
  We will not part from hence. Cesario, come –
  For so you shall be while you are a man,
  But when in other habits you are seen,   380
  Orsino's mistress and his fancy's queen.   381

                      Exeunt [all but the Clown].
                  Clown sings.

  When that I was and a little tiny boy,
    With hey, ho, the wind and the rain,
  A foolish thing was but a toy,
    For the rain it raineth every day.

  But when I came to man's estate,
    With hey, ho, the wind and the rain,
  'Gainst knaves and thieves men shut their gate,
    For the rain it raineth every day.

---

363 *baffled thee* disgraced you publicly 366 *interlude* an early form of dramatic entertainment 370 *whirligig* spinning top or similar toy 375 *convents* is convenient 381 *fancy's* love's

390   But when I came, alas, to wive,
            With hey, ho, the wind and the rain,
392   By swaggering could I never thrive,
            For the rain it raineth every day.

        But when I came unto my beds,
            With hey, ho, the wind and the rain,
396   With tosspots still had drunken heads,
            For the rain it raineth every day.

        A great while ago the world begun,
            With hey, ho, the wind and the rain;
400   But that's all one, our play is done,
            And we'll strive to please you every day.

                                  [Exit.]

---

392 *swaggering* bullying   396 *tosspots* drunkards

FOR THE BEST IN PAPERBACKS, LOOK FOR THE

The distinguished Pelican Shakespeare series, newly revised
to be the premier choice for students, professors, and
general readers well into the 21st century

Antony and Cleopatra
ISBN 0-14-071452-9

The Comedy of Errors
ISBN 0-14-071474-X

Coriolanus
ISBN 0-14-071473-1

Cymbeline
ISBN 0-14-071472-3

Henry IV, Part I
ISBN 0-14-071456-1

Henry IV, Part 2
ISBN 0-14-071457-X

Henry V
ISBN 0-14-071458-8

King Lear
ISBN 0-14-071476-6

King Lear (The Quarto and Folio Texts)
ISBN 0-14-071490-1

Macbeth
ISBN 0-14-071478-2

Much Ado About Nothing
ISBN 0-14-071480-4

The Narrative Poems
ISBN 0-14-071481-2

Richard III
ISBN 0-14-071483-9

Romeo and Juliet
ISBN 0-14-071484-7

The Tempest
ISBN 0-14-071485-5

Timon of Athens
ISBN 0-14-071487-1

Titus Andronicus
ISBN 0-14-071491-X

Twelfth Night
ISBN 0-14-071489-8

The Two Gentlemen of Verona
ISBN 0-14-071461-8

The Winter's Tale
ISBN 0-14-071488-X

All's Well That Ends Well
ISBN 0-14-071460-X

As You Like It
ISBN 0-14-071471-5

Hamlet
ISBN 0-14-071454-5

Henry VI, Part 1
ISBN 0-14-071465-0

Henry VI, Part 2
ISBN 0-14-071466-9

Henry VI, Part 3
ISBN 0-14-071467-7

Henry VIII
ISBN 0-14-071475-8

Julius Caesar
ISBN 0-14-071468-5

King John
ISBN 0-14-071459-6

Love's Labor's Lost
ISBN 0-14-071477-4

Measure for Measure
ISBN 0-14-071479-0

The Merchant of Venice
ISBN 0-14-071462-6

The Merry Wives of Windsor
ISBN 0-14-071464-2

A Midsummer Night's Dream
ISBN 0-14-071455-3

Othello
ISBN 0-14-071463-4

Pericles
ISBN 0-14-071469-3

Richard II
ISBN 0-14-071482-0

The Sonnets
ISBN 0-14-071453-7

The Taming of the Shrew
ISBN 0-14-071451-0

Troilus and Cressida
ISBN 0-14-071486-3

FOR THE BEST IN PAPERBACKS, LOOK FOR THE

In every corner of the world, on every subject under the sun, Penguin represents quality and variety—the very best in publishing today.

For complete information about books available from Penguin—including Penguin Classics, Penguin Compass, and Puffins—and how to order them, write to us at the appropriate address below. Please note that for copyright reasons the selection of books varies from country to country.

In the United States: Please write to *Penguin Group (USA), P.O. Box 12289 Dept. B, Newark, New Jersey 07101-5289* or call 1-800-788-6262.

In the United Kingdom: Please write to *Dept. EP, Penguin Books Ltd, Bath Road, Harmondsworth, West Drayton, Middlesex UB7 0DA.*

In Canada: Please write to *Penguin Books Canada Ltd, 90 Eglinton Avenue East, Suite 700, Toronto, Ontario M4P 2Y3.*

In Australia: Please write to *Penguin Books Australia Ltd, P.O. Box 257, Ringwood, Victoria 3134.*

In New Zealand: Please write to *Penguin Books (NZ) Ltd, Private Bag 102902, North Shore Mail Centre, Auckland 10.*

In India: Please write to *Penguin Books India Pvt Ltd, 11 Panchsheel Shopping Centre, Panchsheel Park, New Delhi 110 017.*

In the Netherlands: Please write to *Penguin Books Netherlands bv, Postbus 3507, NL-1001 AH Amsterdam.*

In Germany: Please write to *Penguin Books Deutschland GmbH, Metzlerstrasse 26, 60594 Frankfurt am Main.*

In Spain: Please write to *Penguin Books S. A., Bravo Murillo 19, 1° B, 28015 Madrid.*

In Italy: Please write to *Penguin Italia s.r.l., Via Benedetto Croce 2, 20094 Corsico, Milano.*

In France: Please write to *Penguin France, Le Carré Wilson, 62 rue Benjamin Baillaud, 31500 Toulouse.*

In Japan: Please write to *Penguin Books Japan Ltd, Kaneko Building, 2-3-25 Koraku, Bunkyo-Ku, Tokyo 112.*

In South Africa: Please write to *Penguin Books South Africa (Pty) Ltd, Private Bag X14, Parkview, 2122 Johannesburg.*